Better Homes and Gardens®

Hometown

FAVORITES

Delicious, down-home recipes

p. 9   p. 38   p. 124   p. 78   p. 173   p. 174

Volume 2

Meredith Consumer Marketing
Des Moines, Iowa

Better Homes and Gardens®
HOMETOWN FAVORITES

Meredith Corporation Consumer Marketing
Vice President, Consumer Marketing: David Ball
Consumer Product Marketing Director: Steve Swanson
Consumer Product Marketing Manager: Wendy Merical
Business Manager: Ron Clingman
Associate Director, Production: Douglas M. Johnston
Photographers: Marty Baldwin, Kritsada Panichgul

Waterbury Publications, Inc.
Editorial Director: Lisa Kingsley
Associate Editor: Tricia Laning
Creative Director: Ken Carlson
Associate Design Director: Doug Samuelson
Production Assistants: Kim Hopkins, Mindy Samuelson
Contributing Food Stylist: Charles Worthington
Contributing Copy Editor: Peg Smith
Contributing Proofreaders: Terri Fredrickson, Gretchen Kauffman
Contributing Indexer: Elizabeth T. Parson

Better Homes and Gardens® **Magazine**
Editor in Chief: Gayle Goodson Butler
Art Director: Michael D. Belknap
Deputy Editor, Food and Entertaining: Nancy Wall Hopkins
Senior Food Editor: Richard Swearinger
Associate Food Editor: Erin Simpson
Editorial Assistant: Renee Irey

Meredith Publishing Group
President: Jack Griffin
Executive Vice President: Andy Sareyan
Vice President, Manufacturing: Bruce Heston

Meredith Corporation
Chairman of the Board: William T. Kerr
President and Chief Executive Officer: Stephen M. Lacy

In Memoriam: E.T. Meredith III (1933–2003)

All of us at Meredith Consumer Marketing are dedicated to providing you with information and ideas to enhance your home. We welcome your comments and suggestions. Write to us at: Meredith Consumer Marketing, 1716 Locust St., Des Moines, IA 50309-3023.

Our Better Homes and Gardens® Test Kitchen seal assures you that every recipe in **Hometown Favorites** has been tested in the Better Homes and Gardens® Test Kitchen. This means that each recipe is practical and reliable, and meets our high standards of taste appeal. We guarantee your satisfaction with this book for as long as you own it.

TABLE OF CONTENTS

p. 7

p. 11

p. 14

p. 19

p. 24

p. 28

4

BOASTFUL BEGINNINGS

RECIPE FINDER

FOR MORE RECIPES:
Visit BHG.com/Recipes

Thai Chicken Wings
with Peanut Sauce, p. 18

Caramel Snack Mix

This crunchy concoction is perfect for parties, a terrific tailgating tote-along, or kid-pleasing after-school snack. In a small bag tied with a pretty ribbon, it's a welcome hostess gift.

PREP: 15 minutes   BAKE: 30 minutes
COOL: 30 minutes   OVEN: 300°F

30 servings	ingredients	15 servings
1 12-oz. box	crispy corn and rice cereal	½ 12-oz. box
1½ cups	mixed nuts, cashews, or almonds	¾ cup
½ cup	packed brown sugar	¼ cup
½ cup	light-color corn syrup	¼ cup
½ cup	butter	¼ cup
2 cups	chocolate-covered raisins, chocolate-covered peanuts, or semisweet or milk chocolate pieces	1 cup

1 Preheat oven to 300°F. In a large roasting pan combine cereal and mixed nuts; set aside.

2 In a saucepan combine brown sugar, corn syrup, and butter. Cook and stir over medium heat until butter is melted and mixture is smooth. Pour over cereal mixture; stir gently to coat.

3 Bake, uncovered, for 30 minutes, stirring twice. Remove from oven. Spread mixture on a large piece of buttered foil; cool for 30 minutes. Break into pieces. Stir in chocolate-covered raisins. Store in an airtight container up to 3 days or freeze up to 1 month.

PER SERVING: 186 cal., 9 g total fat (4 g sat. fat), 9 mg chol., 122 mg sodium, 27 g carbo., 1 g fiber, 2 g pro.

Savory Nuts

To crush the thyme and rosemary, rub the dry herbs between your fingers right before tossing them into the recipe. Crushing releases essential oils in the herbs and intensifies their flavor.

1 Preheat oven to 350°F. Spread nuts in a 13×9×2-inch baking pan. Combine Worcestershire sauce, olive oil, thyme, rosemary, salt, and cayenne pepper; drizzle over nuts. Toss lightly to coat.

2 Bake, uncovered, for 12 to 15 minutes or until nuts are toasted, stirring occasionally. Spread mixture on a large piece of foil; cool for 30 minutes. Store in an airtight container up to 2 weeks.

PER SERVING: 258 cal., 28 g total fat (4 g sat. fat), 0 mg chol., 192 mg sodium, 6 g carbo., 2 g fiber, 2 g pro.

PREP: 5 minutes BAKE: 12 minutes
COOL: 30 minutes OVEN: 350°F

16 servings	ingredients	8 servings
4 cups	assorted nuts (such as macadamia nuts, broken walnuts, and/or unblanched almonds)	2 cups
¼ cup	white wine Worcestershire sauce	2 Tbsp.
2 Tbsp.	olive oil	1 Tbsp.
1 tsp.	dried thyme, crushed	½ tsp.
½ tsp.	dried rosemary, crushed	¼ tsp.
½ tsp.	salt	¼ tsp.
¼ tsp.	cayenne pepper	⅛ tsp.

Creamy Dip for Fruit

Guests appreciate finding healthful options— like this fresh beauty—on appetizer menus. To make the dip lower in fat, use Neufchâtel cheese in place of cream cheese and opt for low-fat sour cream.

1 In a mixing bowl beat cream cheese with an electric mixer on low speed until smooth. Gradually add sour cream, beating until combined. Add brown sugar and vanilla; beat just until combined. Stir in enough milk to make of a dipping consistency. Cover and refrigerate at least 1 hour before serving.

2 To serve, transfer dip to a serving bowl. Serve with assorted fruits.

PER SERVING: 189 cal., 16 g total fat (10 g sat. fat), 44 mg chol., 103 mg sodium, 9 g carbo., 0 g fiber, 3 g pro.

PREP: 15 minutes
CHILL: 1 hour

16 servings	ingredients	8 servings
2 8-oz. pkg.	cream cheese, softened	1 8-oz. pkg.
2 8-oz. cartons	sour cream	1 8-oz. carton
1/2 cup	packed brown sugar	1/4 cup
2 tsp.	vanilla	1 tsp.
4 to 6 Tbsp.	milk	2 to 3 Tbsp.
	Assorted dippers (such as cherries; sliced apples, pears, bananas; and/or strawberries)	

German-Style Dip

This rich, robust dip owes much of its hearty flavor to caraway seeds, common in dishes from Germany, Austria, and Hungary, where it's loved for its nuttiness and licoricelike flavor.

START TO FINISH: 25 minutes

16 servings	ingredients	8 servings
½ cup	finely chopped red onion	¼ cup
2 Tbsp.	olive oil	1 Tbsp.
2 8-oz. pkg.	reduced-fat cream cheese (Neufchâtel), softened	1 8-oz. pkg.
1⅓ cups	light sour cream	⅔ cup
⅓ cup	coarse-grain mustard	3 Tbsp.
1 tsp.	caraway seeds, crushed	½ tsp.
Dash	ground black pepper	Dash
	Assorted dippers (such as red cabbage leaves, roasted potato wedges, cooked bratwurst slices, toasted rye bread, cucumber slices, and/or thinly sliced cooked ham wrapped around mini dill pickles)	

1 In a saucepan cook onion in hot oil over medium-high heat about 4 minutes or until tender. Set aside for 15 minutes to cool.

2 In a mixing bowl beat cream cheese with an electric mixer on medium speed until smooth. Gradually add sour cream, mustard, caraway seeds, and pepper; beat just until combined. Stir in cooled onion.

3 To serve, transfer dip to a serving dish. Serve with assorted dippers. Or cover and refrigerate up to 24 hours. Dip may be thicker after chilling. If necessary, stir in enough milk (1 to 2 tablespoons) to make a dipping consistency.

PER SERVING: 83 cal., 7 g total fat (4 g sat. fat), 18 mg chol., 176 mg sodium, 3 g carbo., 0 g fiber, 2 g pro.

Cheesy Artichoke and Spinach Dip

Stay at home for this rich, hot, and creamy restaurant favorite that makes enough to serve a crowd.

1 Preheat oven to 350°F. In a skillet cook onion, sweet pepper, and garlic in hot oil over medium heat until tender, stirring often. Set aside for 15 minutes to cool.

2 In a bowl stir together cream cheese, Parmesan cheese, milk, mayonnaise, and sour cream. Add cooled onion mixture, spinach, and chopped artichoke hearts; gently stir to combine. For 44 servings, spread mixture into a 3-quart rectangular baking dish or two 1½-quart baking dishes.

3 Bake, uncovered, for 30 to 40 minutes or until bubbly. Serve dip with assorted dippers.

For 22 servings: Prepare using method above, except spread mixture into a deep-dish pie plate or a 1½-quart baking dish.

PER SERVING: 53 cal., 5 g total fat (2 g sat. fat), 11 mg chol., 121 mg sodium, 1 g carbo., 0 g fiber, 2 g pro.

PREP: 25 minutes   BAKE: 30 minutes
COOL: 15 minutes   OVEN: 350°F

44 servings	ingredients	22 servings
½ cup	chopped onion	¼ cup
½ cup	chopped red sweet pepper	¼ cup
2 cloves	garlic, minced	1 clove
1 Tbsp.	olive oil	1½ tsp.
2 8-oz. pkgs.	reduced-fat cream cheese (Neufchâtel), softened	1 8-oz. pkg.
1½ cups	finely shredded Parmesan or Romano cheese	¾ cup
¼ cup	milk	2 Tbsp.
¼ cup	mayonnaise	2 Tbsp.
¼ cup	light sour cream	2 Tbsp.
4 cups	chopped fresh spinach leaves	2 cups
1 14-oz. can	artichoke hearts, drained and chopped	½ 14-oz. can
	Assorted dippers (such as sliced toasted baguette-style French bread, bagel chips, and/or corn tortilla chips)	

White Bean Dip

It is highly unlikely that you will have any of this Italian-inspired dip left over—it's that good. If you do, use some as a sandwich spread with roast beef and tomatoes on a crisp baguette.

PREP: 20 minutes
CHILL: 4 hours

16 servings	ingredients	8 servings
¹⁄₄ cup	soft bread crumbs	2 Tbsp.
2 Tbsp.	dry white wine or water	1 Tbsp.
1 19-oz. can	cannellini (white kidney) beans, rinsed and drained	¹⁄₂ 19-oz. can
¹⁄₄ cup	slivered almonds, toasted	2 Tbsp.
2 to 3 cloves	garlic, minced	1 to 2 cloves
2 Tbsp.	lemon juice	1 Tbsp.
2 Tbsp.	olive oil	1 Tbsp.
¹⁄₄ tsp.	salt	¹⁄₈ tsp.
¹⁄₈ tsp.	cayenne pepper	Dash
2 tsp.	snipped fresh oregano or basil or ¹⁄₂ the amount of dried oregano or basil, crushed	1 tsp.
	Fresh oregano or basil leaves (optional)	
	Toasted pita chips or assorted vegetable dippers (such as broccoli florets, carrot sticks, and/or yellow pepper strips)	

1 In a bowl combine bread crumbs and wine; set aside for 10 minutes to soak.

2 Meanwhile, in a food processor or blender combine drained cannellini beans, almonds, garlic, lemon juice, olive oil, salt, and cayenne pepper. Cover and process or blend until almost smooth. Add bread crumb mixture; cover and process or blend until smooth. Transfer dip to a serving bowl. Stir in the snipped oregano. Cover and refrigerate for 4 to 24 hours.

3 To serve, if desired, garnish dip with fresh oregano leaves. Serve with toasted pita chips and/or vegetable dippers.

PER SERVING: 50 cal., 3 g total fat (0 g sat. fat), 0 mg chol., 93 mg sodium, 6 g carbo., 2 g fiber, 2 g pro.

Supreme Pizza Fondue

Italian sausage is available in two versions—hot, which is spiced up with hot peppers, and mild, which is heat free. The mild variety is sometimes called "sweet" Italian sausage.

START TO FINISH: 25 minutes

16 servings	ingredients	8 servings
4 oz.	bulk Italian sausage	2 oz.
1/3 cup	small onion, finely chopped	3 Tbsp.
1 clove	garlic, minced	1/2 clove
1 26-oz. jar	spaghetti sauce	1/2 26-oz. jar
1 cup	chopped fresh mushrooms	1/2 cup
2/3 cup	chopped pepperoni or Canadian-style bacon	1/3 cup
1 tsp.	dried basil or oregano, crushed	1/2 tsp.
1/2 cup	chopped pitted ripe olives (optional)	1/4 cup
1/4 cup	finely chopped green sweet pepper (optional)	2 Tbsp.
	Assorted dippers (such as Italian bread cubes, cooked tortellini, and/or mozzarella or provolone cheese cubes)	

1 In a skillet cook the sausage, onion, and garlic over medium-high heat until meat is browned. Drain off fat.

2 Add spaghetti sauce, mushrooms, pepperoni, and basil. Heat to boiling; reduce heat. Simmer, covered, for 10 minutes. If desired, stir in ripe olives and sweet pepper. Simmer, covered, about 5 minutes more or until sweet pepper is tender.

3 To serve, transfer sausage mixture to a fondue pot; keep warm over a fondue burner. Serve with assorted dippers.

PER SERVING: 59 cal., 4 g total fat (2 g sat. fat), 10 mg chol., 296 mg sodium, 3 g carbo., 1 g fiber, 3 g pro.

Double-Quick Shrimp Cocktail

Talk about a triple play! This simple starter pleases shrimp lovers and dazzles those who adore a creamy dip as well as the piquant red classic.

1 In a bowl combine sour cream, horseradish, snipped chives, and lemon juice. If desired, cover and refrigerate up to 4 hours before serving.

2 To serve, transfer sour cream mixture to a shallow serving dish. Pour seafood cocktail sauce into another serving dish. Place both serving dishes on a large serving platter. Arrange shrimp around dishes. Serve with chives and/or lemon slices or wedges.

PER SERVING: 37 cal., 1 g total fat (1 g sat. fat), 36 mg chol., 119 mg sodium, 2 g carbo., 0 g fiber, 4 g pro.

START TO FINISH: 15 minutes

40 servings	ingredients	20 servings
1 8-oz. carton	sour cream	½ 8-oz. carton
¼ cup	prepared horseradish	2 Tbsp.
2 Tbsp.	snipped chives or thinly sliced green onion tops	1 Tbsp.
1 Tbsp.	lemon juice	1½ tsp.
1 12-oz. jar	seafood cocktail sauce or chili sauce	½ 12-oz. jar
1½ lb. (60 to 75)	frozen peeled and cooked shrimp with tails, thawed	¾ lb. (30 to 38)
	Chives and/or lemon slices or wedges	

Buffalo-Style Chicken Fingers

This version of Buffalo wings is the healthful way to go. A serving of this recipe contains half the calories and two-thirds less fat than the same serving size of traditional Buffalo wings.

PREP: 25 minutes
BAKE: 18 minutes
OVEN: 425°F

24 servings	ingredients	12 servings
4 cups	crushed cornflakes	2 cups
¼ cup	finely snipped parsley	2 Tbsp.
1 tsp.	salt	½ tsp.
2 lb.	skinless, boneless chicken breast halves	1 lb.
⅔ cup	bottled blue cheese salad dressing	⅓ cup
4 tsp.	water	2 tsp.
2 to 4 tsp.	bottled hot pepper sauce	1 to 2 tsp.
	Celery sticks	
	Bottled blue cheese salad dressing	

1 Preheat oven to 425°F. In a shallow bowl or pie plate combine crushed cornflakes, parsley, and salt. Cut chicken breasts into strips about ¾ inch wide and 3 inches long.

2 For 24 servings, in a bowl combine the ⅔ cup blue cheese salad dressing, the water, and hot pepper sauce. Add chicken; stir to coat. Roll each chicken piece in cornflake mixture to coat.

3 Place chicken strips in a single layer in two lightly greased 15×10×1-inch baking pans. Bake, one pan at a time, for 18 to 20 minutes or until chicken is no longer pink and coating is golden.

4 To serve, transfer chicken strips to a serving platter. Serve warm with celery sticks and additional blue cheese dressing for dipping.

For 12 servings: Prepare using method above, except in a bowl combine the ⅓ cup blue cheese salad dressing, the water, and hot pepper sauce. Place chicken strips in a single layer in a lightly greased 15×10×1-inch baking pan.

PER SERVING: 184 cal., 12 g total fat (2 g sat. fat), 26 mg chol., 408 mg sodium, 9 g carbo., 0 g fiber, 11 g pro.

Thai Chicken Wings with Peanut Sauce

When peeling ginger, be careful to remove only the thin brown skin—the delicate flesh immedietely beneath the surface is most flavorful. For easy grating, first freeze ginger for 15 minutes.

PREP: 25 minutes **BAKE:** 20 minutes
OVEN: 400°F

12 servings	ingredients	6 servings
2¼ lb. (about 20)	chicken wing drummettes	1 lb. (about 10)
½ cup	salsa	¼ cup
2 Tbsp.	creamy peanut butter	1 Tbsp.
1 Tbsp.	lime juice	1½ tsp.
2 tsp.	soy sauce	1 tsp.
2 tsp.	grated fresh ginger	1 tsp.
¼ cup	sugar	2 Tbsp.
¼ cup	creamy peanut butter	2 Tbsp.
3 Tbsp.	soy sauce	4½ tsp.
3 Tbsp.	water	4½ tsp.
2 cloves	garlic, minced	1 clove
	Shredded bok choy (optional)	
	Lime wedges (optional)	

1 Preheat oven to 400°F. Place drummettes in a large bowl. For 12 servings, combine salsa, the 2 tablespoons peanut butter, lime juice, the 2 teaspoons soy sauce, and ginger. Pour over drummettes, tossing to coat.

2 Arrange drummettes in a single layer in a baking pan or roasting pan lined with foil. Bake, uncovered, about 20 minutes or until tender and no longer pink.

3 Meanwhile, for the peanut sauce, in a saucepan combine the sugar, the ¼ cup peanut butter, the 3 tablespoons soy sauce, the water, and garlic. Cook and stir over medium-low heat until sugar is dissolved and mixture is smooth.

4 To serve, transfer warm drummettes to a serving platter and pour peanut sauce into serving bowl. (Sauce will thicken as it stands.) If desired, garnish with shredded bok choy and lime wedges.

For 6 servings: Prepare using method above, except combine salsa, the 1 tablespoon peanut butter, lime juice, 1 teaspoon soy sauce, and ginger. For the peanut sauce, in a saucepan combine sugar, the 2 tablespoons peanut butter, the 4½ teaspoons soy sauce, the water, and garlic.

PER SERVING: 189 cal., 13 g total fat (3 g sat. fat), 58 mg chol., 392 mg sodium, 6 g carbo., 1 g fiber, 12 g pro.

Mushroom-Bacon Turnovers

The meaty flesh of shiitake (shee-TAH-kay) mushrooms is gutsy and robust—almost like steak—in flavor. The stems, however, are tough, so use only the caps in this recipe.

1 Preheat oven to 350°F. For filling, in a skillet melt butter over medium heat. Add mushrooms and onion. Cook about 5 minutes or until mushrooms are tender, stirring occasionally. Stir in whipping cream. Simmer, uncovered, for 2 minutes more. Remove skillet from heat. Stir in bacon, thyme, and basil.

2 Using your fingers, separate each biscuit in half so you have 32 biscuit rounds. On a lightly floured surface, use the palm of your hand to flatten each biscuit round to a 3-inch circle. Place about 2 teaspoons of the filling onto one-half of each circle of dough. Fold dough over filling; seal edges by pressing them together firmly with tines of a fork. Place filled turnovers on two ungreased baking sheets.

3 In a bowl beat eggs with a whisk; brush egg over turnovers. Bake, one sheet at a time, for 14 to 17 minutes or until turnovers are golden. Serve warm.

For 16 servings: Prepare using method above, except, using your fingers, separate each biscuit in half for 16 biscuit rounds.

PER SERVING: 139 cal., 8 g total fat (3 g sat. fat), 22 mg chol., 310 mg sodium, 13 g carbo., 1 g fiber, 3 g pro.

PREP: 30 minutes   BAKE: 14 minutes
OVEN: 350°F

32 servings	ingredients	16 servings
1/4 cup	butter or margarine	2 Tbsp.
4 cups	chopped fresh brown or button mushrooms	2 cups
2 cups	chopped fresh shiitake mushrooms (caps only)	1 cup
2/3 cup	finely chopped red onion	1/3 cup
1/3 cup	whipping cream	3 Tbsp.
6 slices	bacon, crisp-cooked, drained, and crumbled	3 slices
2 Tbsp.	snipped fresh thyme	1 Tbsp.
2 Tbsp.	snipped fresh basil	1 Tbsp.
2 17.3-oz. pkg. (16)	refrigerated large biscuits	1 17.3-oz. pkg. (8)
2	egg(s)	1

Date-Sausage Bites

Rarely you'll happen across a food pairing that's a match made in heaven. Dates and sausages are just such a marriage of wonderful flavors: sweetness from the dates and savory saltiness from the sausage.

1 Preheat oven to 400°F. Carefully unfold the pastry. Cut along folds, making 6 rectangles; set aside.

2 For filling, in a bowl combine sausage, dates, garlic powder, sage, red pepper, and black pepper. Spread abut ¼ cup filling lengthwise along half of each pastry rectangle to within ½ inch of one long edge. Fold the opposite side of pastry over meat mixture; pinch edges to seal. Cut filled pastries into 1-inch pieces. For 24 servings, place the pieces, pastry sides down, on two ungreased 15×10×1-inch baking pans.

3 Bake, one pan at a time, about 20 minutes or until golden brown. Serve warm.

For 12 servings: Prepare using method above, except cut along folds, making 3 rectangles; set aside. Place the pieces, pastry sides down, on one ungreased 15×10×1-inch baking pan.

PER SERVING: 75 cal., 5 g total fat (1 g sat. fat), 4 mg chol., 76 mg sodium, 6 g carbo., 0 g fiber, 1 g pro.

PREP: 25 minutes
BAKE: 20 minutes
OVEN: 400°F

24 servings	ingredients	12 servings
1 17.3-oz. pkg. (2 sheets)	frozen puff pastry, thawed	½ 17.3-oz. pkg. (1 sheet)
12 oz.	maple-flavored bulk pork sausage	6 oz.
1 cup	chopped pitted dates	½ cup
1 tsp.	garlic powder	½ tsp.
½ tsp.	dried sage or oregano, crushed	¼ tsp.
¼ tsp.	crushed red pepper	⅛ tsp.
¼ tsp.	ground black pepper	⅛ tsp.

Spicy Spinach-Stuffed Mushrooms

For a beautiful buffet presentation—and to keep mushrooms from sliding on the serving platter—place the caps on a bed of shredded spinach or warmed rock salt.

1 Preheat oven to 425°F. Rinse and drain mushrooms. Remove stems and chop; set aside. Brush mushroom caps with olive oil. Sprinkle with salt and black pepper. Set aside.

2 For filling, in a skillet cook chopped stems, sausage, onion, sweet pepper, and garlic over medium heat until sausage is browned. Stir in spinach until wilted. Stir in Parmesan cheese and bread crumbs. Remove from heat. Spoon sausage mixture into mushroom caps. Place, filled sides up, on a greased baking sheet.

3 Bake, uncovered, for 10 to 12 minutes or until stuffing is golden brown and mushrooms are tender.

PER SERVING: 53 cal., 4 g total fat (2 g sat. fat), 7 mg chol., 179 mg sodium, 2 g carbo., 0 g fiber, 3 g pro.

PREP: 30 minutes
BAKE: 10 minutes
OVEN: 425°F

24 servings	ingredients	12 servings
24 large	fresh mushrooms, 1½ to 2 inches in diameter	12 large
2 Tbsp.	olive oil	1 Tbsp.
	Salt	
	Ground black pepper	
8 oz.	spicy bulk Italian sausage	4 oz.
¼ cup	finely chopped onion	2 Tbsp.
¼ cup	finely chopped red sweet pepper	2 Tbsp.
2 cloves	garlic, minced	1 clove
1 cup	fresh spinach, chopped	½ cup
¼ cup	finely shredded Parmesan cheese	2 Tbsp.
¼ cup	fine dry bread crumbs	2 Tbsp.

Sweet and Sassy Meatballs

These roly-poly orbs of goodness are so easy that a child can make them. Invite one of the kids to join you in the kitchen for some fun.

START TO FINISH: 20 minutes

64 servings	ingredients	32 servings
1 18-oz. bottle	barbecue sauce	½ 18-oz. bottle
1 16-oz. bottle	jellied cranberry sauce	½ 16-oz. bottle
2 1-lb. pkg. (64 total)	frozen cooked meatballs, thawed	1 1-lb. pkg. (32 total)

1 For sauce, in a skillet combine barbecue sauce and cranberry sauce. Cook over medium heat until cranberry sauce is melted, stirring occasionally.

2 Add meatballs to sauce. Cook, uncovered, for 10 minutes or until meatballs are heated through, stirring occasionally.

3 To serve, transfer to a chafing dish or slow cooker; keep warm.

PER SERVING: 60 cal., 4 g total fat (2 g sat. fat), 5 mg chol., 177 mg sodium, 5 g carbo., 1 g fiber, 2 g pro.

Plum-Good Sausage and Meatballs

If you are lucky enough to have any party leftovers, serve these saucy meatballs and sausages over hot cooked rice for a family-friendly main dish.

PREP: 10 minutes
COOK: 5 to 6 hours (low)
or 2½ to 3 hours (high)

32 servings	ingredients	16 servings
2 10-oz. or 12-oz. jars	plum jam or preserves	1 10-oz. or 12-oz. jar
2 18-oz. bottles	barbecue sauce	1 18-oz. bottle
2 16-oz. pkg.	cooked jalapeño smoked sausage or smoked sausage, sliced in bite-size pieces	1 16-oz. pkg.
2 16-oz. to 18-oz. pkg.	Italian-style or regular frozen cooked meatballs, thawed	1 16-oz. to 18-oz. pkg.

1 For 32 servings, in a 5- to 6-quart slow cooker combine jam, barbecue sauce, sausage, and thawed meatballs.

2 Cover and cook on low-heat setting for 5 to 6 hours or on high-heat setting for 2½ to 3 hours.

3 Serve immediately or keep warm on warm setting or low-heat setting up to 2 hours. Stir occasionally.

For 16 servings: Prepare using method above, except use a 3½- to 4-quart slow cooker.

PER SERVING: 267 cal., 16 g total fat (6 g sat. fat), 38 mg chol., 898 mg sodium, 19 g carbo., 2 g fiber, 12 g pro.

Spicy Cajun Shrimp

There are many Cajun seasonings on the market today, each with distinct characteristics. Most of these sassy blends, however, share common ingredients: garlic, onion, chiles, pepper, and mustard and celery seeds.

START TO FINISH: 25 minutes

32 servings	ingredients	16 servings
2 lb.	fresh or frozen large shrimp in shells	1 lb.
1 cup	mayonnaise or salad dressing	½ cup
¼ cup	tomato paste	2 Tbsp.
2 Tbsp.	lemon juice	1 Tbsp.
2 cloves	garlic, minced	1 clove
¼ cup	butter or margarine, melted	2 Tbsp.
2 Tbsp.	Cajun seasoning	3 tsp.

1 Thaw shrimp, if frozen. Peel and devein shrimp, leaving tails intact, if desired. Rinse shrimp; pat dry with paper towels; set aside.

2 For sauce, in a bowl combine mayonnaise, tomato paste, lemon juice, and garlic. Cover and refrigerate until ready to serve.

3 Preheat broiler. Brush both sides of each shrimp with melted butter. Sprinkle both sides of each shrimp with Cajun seasoning. Place shrimp on the unheated rack of a broiler pan.

4 Broil 4 to 5 inches from heat for 2 minutes. Turn shrimp; broil for 1 to 2 minutes more or until shrimp are opaque. Serve shrimp with sauce.

PER SERVING: 181 cal., 15 g total fat (3 g sat. fat), 83 mg chol., 264 mg sodium, 2 g carbo., 0 g fiber, 9 g pro.

Crab and Horseradish-Havarti Dip

Havarti is a pale yellow semisoft Danish cheese. Riddled with small "eyes" like Swiss cheese and wrapped in a reddish rind, it boasts a mild, yet tangy flavor—and a texture that makes this dip luxuriously creamy.

1 Preheat oven to 350°F. In a large bowl combine cream cheese, 2 cups of the Havarti cheese, the sour cream, and mayonnaise; beat with an electric mixer on medium speed until well mixed. Gently stir in crabmeat and spinach.

2 For 24 servings, transfer mixture to a 2-quart baking dish. Bake about 25 minutes or until bubbly and heated through. Sprinkle with the remaining Havarti cheese and the green onions. Serve with assorted breads.

To make 12 servings: Prepare using method above, except assemble and bake in one 1-quart baking dish.

*Note: If you can't find horseradish and chive Havarti cheese, substitute 2½ cups shredded Havarti and add 2 tablespoons snipped fresh chives and 4 teaspoons prepared horseradish with the sour cream.

PER SERVING: 181 cal., 15 g total fat (3 g sat. fa)t, 83 mg chol., 264 mg sodium, 2 g carbo., 0 g fiber, 9 g pro.

**PREP: 15 minutes BAKE: 25 minutes
OVEN: 350°F**

24 servings	ingredients	12 servings
2 8 oz. pkg.	cream cheese, softened	1 8 oz. pkg.
2½ cups	shredded horseradish and chive Havarti cheese* (5 oz.)	1¼ cups
⅔ cups	sour cream	⅓ cup
½ cup	mayonnaise	¼ cup
2 cups	cooked crabmeat or one 6-ounce can crabmeat, drained, flaked, and cartilage removed	1 cup
2 cups	shredded fresh baby spinach	1 cup
⅔ cup	thinly sliced green onions	⅓ cup
	Flatbread, bagel chips, crostini, and/or toasted baguette-style French bread slcies	

p. 33

p. 43

p. 53

p. 60

p. 70

p. 73

30

FAVORITE POULTRY DISHES

RECIPE FINDER

FOR MORE RECIPES:
Visit BHG.com/Recipes

Chicken and Orzo Casserole, p.52

Crunchy Chicken Salad

If your mother served chicken salad studded with peanut brittle, you might have worked your way into Clean Plate Club more quickly.

PREP: 20 minutes
CHILL: 2 to 24 hours

6 servings	ingredients	4 servings
4 cups (about 1¼ lb.)	coarsely shredded cooked chicken	3 cups (about 15 oz.)
1⅓ cups	coarsely chopped celery	1 cup
⅔ cup	mayonnaise or salad dressing	½ cup
½ cup	finely chopped onion	⅓ cup
4 tsp.	olive oil	1 Tbsp.
¼ tsp.	salt	¼ tsp.
¼ tsp.	ground black pepper	¼ tsp.
1 cup	broken peanut brittle	¾ cup
⅔ cup	salted mixed nuts, coarsely chopped	½ cup
	Flatbread (optional)	

1 In a large bowl stir together chicken, celery, mayonnaise, onion, oil, salt, and pepper. Cover and refrigerate* for 2 to 24 hours.

2 Stir in peanut brittle and nuts just before serving. If desired, serve with flatbread.

*Note: Salad can be chilled up to 2 hours after adding the peanut brittle and nuts.

PER SERVING: 605 cal., 43 g total fat (7 g sat. fat), 104 mg chol., 572 mg sodium, 7 g carbo., 2 g fiber, 35 g pro.

Chicken-and-Grape Pasta Salad

To make this colorful creation even easier to prepare, pick up one of a busy cook's greatest conveniences—ready-to-go deli rotisserie chicken.

1 Cook pasta according to package directions. Drain pasta. Rinse with cold water. Drain again.

2 In a large salad bowl combine pasta, chicken, grapes, strawberries, and jicama.

3 For dressing, combine dressing and pepper. Pour dressing over chicken mixture. Toss lightly to coat. Cover and refrigerate for 4 to 24 hours.

4 Before serving, if necessary, stir in milk, 1 tablespoon at a time, until salad is creamy. If desired, sprinkle with sugared almonds.

PER SERVING: 455 cal., 20 g total fat (3 g sat. fat), 57 mg chol., 269 mg sodium, 43 g carbo., 3 g fiber, 27 g pro.

PREP: 40 minutes
CHILL: 4 to 24 hours

12 servings	ingredients	6 servings
3 cups	dried radiatore, mostaccioli, and/or medium shell pasta	1½ cups
6 cups (about 1¾ lb.)	chopped cooked chicken	3 cups (about 15 oz.)
6 cups	fresh seedless grapes, halved	3 cups
3 cups	small strawberries, halved	1½ cups
2 cups	chopped, peeled jicama	1 cup
1⅓ cups	bottled cucumber ranch salad dressing	⅔ cup
¼ tsp.	cayenne pepper	⅛ tsp.
	Milk (optional)	
	Purchased sugared sliced almonds (optional)	

Chicken-Cabbage Salad

The thin, crinkly cream-color leaves of napa cabbage—also called Chinese cabbage—give this Asian-inspired salad delicate flavor, but other cabbages make it crunchier. The choice is yours.

1 Preheat oven to 350°F. Save seasoning packet(s) from noodles for another use. Break up the noodles. On a large baking sheet combine noodles, almonds, and sesame seeds. Bake for 5 to 8 minutes or until golden, stirring once. Cool on a wire rack.

2 In a large salad bowl toss together cabbage, chicken, pea pods, green onions, and, if desired, sweet pepper.

3 For dressing, in a screw-top jar combine vegetable oil, vinegar, soy sauce, sugar, and, if desired, sesame oil. Cover and shake well. Pour over cabbage mixture. Add toasted noodle mixture; toss to coat. Serve immediately.

PER SERVING: 435 cal., 27 g total fat (4 g sat. fat), 63 mg chol., 517 mg sodium, 21 g carbo., 4 g fiber, 28 g pro.

PREP: 20 minutes
BAKE: 5 minutes
OVEN: 350°F

8 servings	ingredients	4 servings
2 3-oz. pkg.	ramen noodles	1 3-oz. pkg.
½ cup	slivered or sliced almonds	¼ cup
¼ cup	sesame seeds	2 Tbsp.
6 cups	shredded napa cabbage or round head cabbage	3 cups
4 cups (about 1¼ lb.)	chopped cooked chicken or turkey	2 cups (about 10 oz.)
2 cups	pea pods, halved crosswise	1 cup
½ cup	thinly sliced green onions	¼ cup
½ cup	chopped red sweet pepper (optional)	¼ cup
6 Tbsp.	vegetable oil	3 Tbsp.
¼ cup	white wine vinegar or rice vinegar	2 Tbsp.
¼ cup	soy sauce	2 Tbsp.
2 tsp.	sugar	1 tsp.
1 tsp.	toasted sesame oil (optional)	½ tsp.

Curried Pasta-and-Chicken Salad

Widely used in Indian cooking, curry powder is a mixture of up to 20 spices. Whether you choose regular curry powder or the hotter Madras curry powder, buy it in small quantities—it keeps its flavor for only 2 months.

PREP: 25 minutes
CHILL: 4 to 24 hours

9 servings	ingredients	6 servings
3 cups (12 oz.)	dried radiatore or rotini pasta	2 cups (8 oz.)
3 cups (about 15 oz.)	cubed cooked chicken	2 cups (about 10 oz.)
2¼ cups	seedless green grapes, halved	1½ cups
2¼ cups	cubed cantaloupe	1½ cups
1¼ cups	sliced celery	¾ cup
¾ cup	sliced green onions	½ cup
¼ cup	chutney	3 Tbsp.
1½ cups	plain low-fat yogurt	1 cup
2¼ tsp.	curry powder	1½ tsp.
½ tsp.	salt	¼ tsp.
	Milk (optional)	

1 Cook pasta according to package directions. Drain; rinse with cold water. Drain again.

2 In a bowl combine pasta, chicken, grapes, cantaloupe, celery, and green onions.

3 For dressing, cut up any large pieces in the chutney. In a bowl stir together chutney, yogurt, curry powder, and salt. Pour dressing over pasta mixture. Toss to coat. Cover and refrigerate for 4 to 24 hours.

4 Before serving, if necessary, stir in milk, 1 tablespoon at a time, until salad is creamy.

PER SERVING: 314 cal., 5 g total fat (2 g sat. fat), 44 mg chol., 204 mg sodium, 46 g carbo., 3 g fiber, 21 g pro.

Creamy Hot Chicken Salad

Looking for the perfect dish to tote to potlucks? Look no further. Time after time this bubbly beauty attracts the most enthusiastic eaters.

1 Preheat oven to 400°F. In a bowl stir together chicken, soup, celery, sweet peppers, yogurt, cheese, green onions, lemon juice, and black pepper. For 12 servings, divide mixture between two 2-quart rectangular baking dishes.

2 In a bowl stir together cornflakes and almonds. Sprinkle evenly over chicken mixture in baking dish(es).

3 Bake, uncovered, about 30 minutes or until heated through. Let stand for 10 minutes before serving.

For 6 servings: Prepare using method above, except assemble and bake in one 2-quart rectangular baking dish.

PER SERVING: 251 cal., 9 g total fat (4 g sat. fat), 75 mg chol., 415 mg sodium, 13 g carbo., 2 g fiber, 29 g pro.

PREP: 20 minutes BAKE: 30 minutes
STAND: 10 minutes OVEN: 400°F

12 servings	ingredients	6 servings
6 cups (about 1³/₄ lb.)	cubed cooked chicken breast	3 cups (about 15 oz.)
2 10.75-oz. cans	reduced-fat and reduced-sodium condensed cream of chicken soup	1 10.75-oz. can
2 cups	sliced celery	1 cup
2 cups	chopped yellow or red sweet peppers	1 cup
2 6-oz. cartons	plain low-fat yogurt	1 6-oz. carton
1¹/₂ cups (6 oz.)	shredded reduced-fat cheddar or mozzarella cheese	³/₄ cup (3 oz.)
¹/₂ cup	sliced green onions	¹/₄ cup
2 Tbsp.	lemon juice	1 Tbsp.
¹/₂ tsp.	ground black pepper	¹/₄ tsp.
1 cup	crushed cornflakes	¹/₂ cup
¹/₂ cup	sliced almonds	¹/₄ cup

Cheesy Corn-and-Chicken Turnovers

Impress family and friends with this easy—and amazingly tasty—version of Latin empanadas. The light and flaky crust surrounds the hearty fillings in the little pies.

PREP: 35 minutes
BAKE: 15 minutes
OVEN: 400°F

8 servings	ingredients	4 servings
4 cups (about 1¼ lb.)	chopped cooked chicken	2 cups (about 10 oz.)
2 11-oz. cans	whole kernel corn with sweet peppers, drained	1 11-oz. can
2 10.75-oz. cans	condensed cream of chicken with herbs soup or cream of mushroom soup	1 10.75-oz. can
2 cups (8 oz.)	shredded cheddar cheese	1 cup (4 oz.)
2 15-ounce pkg. (2 crusts each)	rolled refrigerated unbaked piecrust	1 15-oz. pkg. (2 crusts)
	Water	

1 Preheat oven to 400°F. For 8 servings, grease two large baking sheets; set aside. In a bowl combine chicken, corn, soup, and cheese. Unroll piecrusts according to package directions. On a lightly floured surface, roll each piecrust to a 13-inch circle. Cut each crust in fourths. Spoon about ½ cup of the chicken mixture along one straight side of each quarter, about ¾ inch from the edge.

2 Brush edges of pastry fourths with water. Fold the opposite straight side of each fourths over the filling. Seal edges with tines of a fork and prick the top of each turnover several times. Place turnovers on prepared baking sheet(s). Bake about 15 minutes or until turnovers are golden. Serve hot.

For 4 servings: Prepare using method above, except bake turnovers on one large baking sheet.

PER SERVING: 862 cal., 47 g total fat (21 g sat. fat), 118 mg chol., 1,625 mg sodium, 73 g carbo., 3 g fiber, 33 g pro.

Chicken and Stuffing Casserole

This luscious dish is like a Thanksgiving feast—all in one dish. Substitute turkey for the chicken if you wish, and for the full effect, serve it with cranberry sauce on the side.

1 For 16 servings, in a large skillet heat butter over medium heat. Add celery and onion; cook and stir about 5 minutes or until vegetables are tender. Set aside.

2 Lightly coat a $5^1/_2$- to 6-quart slow cooker with cooking spray. Add rice mix (set aside seasoning packet). Using a slotted spoon, transfer celery and onion to cooker, reserving butter in skillet. Stir to combine.

3 Place croutons in a very large bowl. Stir in butter from skillet; add chicken, mushrooms, parsley, poultry seasoning, pepper, and seasoning packet from rice mix.

4 In a bowl combine egg(s), broth, and soup. Pour over crouton mixture; toss gently to moisten. Transfer to cooker.

5 Cover and cook on low-heat setting for $4^1/_2$ to 5 hours. Stir gently before serving.

For 8 to 10 servings: Prepare using method above, except use a $3^1/_2$- or 4-quart slow cooker. In Step 3, use half of the seasoning packet from the rice mix.

PER SERVING: 287 cal., 11 g total fat (5 g sat. fat), 76 mg chol., 903 mg sodium, 31 g carbo., 3 g fiber, 16 g pro.

PREP: 30 minutes
COOK: $4^1/_2$ to 5 hours (low)

16 servings	ingredients	8 servings
$^1/_2$ cup	butter or margarine	$^1/_4$ cup
1 cup	thinly sliced celery	$^1/_2$ cup
$^3/_4$ cup	chopped onion	$^1/_2$ cup
	Nonstick cooking spray	
1 6-oz. pkg.	long grain and wild rice mix	$^1/_2$ 6-oz. pkg.
1 14-oz. pkg.	herb-seasoned stuffing croutons	$^1/_2$ 14-oz. pkg.
4 cups (about $1^1/_4$ lb.)	cubed cooked chicken	2 cups (about 10 oz.)
2 4-oz. cans	(drained weight) sliced mushrooms, drained	1 4-oz. can
$^1/_4$ cup	snipped fresh parsley	2 Tbsp.
$1^1/_2$ tsp.	poultry seasoning	$^3/_4$ tsp.
$^1/_4$ tsp.	ground black pepper	$^1/_8$ tsp.
2	egg(s), slightly beaten	1
2 14-oz. cans	reduced-sodium chicken broth	1 14-oz. can
1 10.75-oz. can	reduced-fat and reduced-sodium condensed cream of chicken soup or cream of mushroom soup	$^1/_2$ 10.75-oz. can

Chicken Enchiladas

Count on this creamy-rich adaptation of Mexico's famous enchiladas suizas to deliver south-of-the-border warmth to your table— whatever the season.

PREP: 35 minutes
BAKE: 40 minutes OVEN: 350°F

12 servings	ingredients	6 servings
¼ cup	butter or margarine	2 Tbsp.
½ cup	slivered almonds	¼ cup
½ cup	chopped onion	¼ cup
2 4-oz. cans	diced green chile peppers, drained	1 4-oz. can
2 3-oz. pkg.	cream cheese, softened	1 3-oz. pkg.
2 Tbsp.	milk	1 Tbsp.
½ tsp.	ground cumin	¼ tsp.
4 cups (about 1¼ lb.)	chopped cooked chicken or turkey	2 cups (about 10 oz.)
24 7-inch	flour tortillas or 6-inch corn tortillas	12 7-inch
2 10.75-oz. cans	reduced-fat and reduced-sodium condensed cream of chicken soup or cream of mushroom soup	1 10.75-oz. can
2 8-oz. cartons	light sour cream	1 8-oz. carton
2 cups	milk	1 cup
1½ cups (6 oz.)	shredded Monterey Jack or cheddar cheese	¾ cup (3 oz.)

1 Preheat oven to 350°F. For 12 servings, grease two 3-quart rectangular baking dishes; set aside. In a medium skillet melt the butter over medium heat. Cook the almonds and the onion in hot butter until onion is tender and nuts are lightly toasted. Remove from heat. Stir in 2 tablespoons of the chile peppers; reserve remaining peppers for sauce.

2 In a bowl stir together cream cheese, the 2 tablespoons milk, and the cumin; add nut mixture and chicken. Stir until combined. Spoon about 3 tablespoons of the chicken mixture onto each tortilla near an edge; roll up. Place filled tortillas, seam sides down, in prepared baking dishes. Set aside.

3 For sauce, in a bowl combine the reserved chile peppers, the soup, sour cream, and the 2 cups milk. Evenly pour over the tortillas in the baking dishes. Cover with foil.

4 Bake about 35 minutes or until heated through. Remove foil. Sprinkle enchiladas with cheese. Return to oven; bake about 5 minutes more or until cheese is melted.

For 6 servings: Prepare using the method above, except assemble and bake in one 3-quart rectangular baking dish. In Step 1 cook 4 tablespoons almonds with the onion and stir 1 tablespoon chile peppers into the nut mixture. In Step 2 use 1 tablespoon milk in the chicken mixture. In Step 3 use 1 cup milk to make the sauce.

PER SERVING: 538 cal., 30 g total fat (13 g sat. fat), 100 mg chol., 635 mg sodium, 38 g carbo., 3 g fiber, 29 g pro.

Greek Chicken-and-Pita Bake

Kalamata olives—rich, fruity, and meaty—and tangy, salty feta cheese imbue this bright, healthful casserole with sun-drenched Mediterranean flavors.

1 Preheat oven to 350°F. In a bowl combine chicken, zucchini, soup, broth, onion, garlic, and Greek seasoning. For 8 servings, divide mixture between two 3-quart rectangular baking dishes. Cover with foil. Bake for 30 minutes or until vegetables are almost tender.

2 In a bowl toss together pita bread pieces, cheese, olives, and oil. Uncover baking dishes; stir chicken mixture. Sprinkle pita bread mixture and tomatoes over chicken mixture. Bake, uncovered, about 20 minutes more or until top is golden.

For 4 servings: Prepare using method above, except assemble and bake in one 3-quart rectangular baking dish.

PER SERVING: 468 cal., 22 g total fat (8 g sat. fat), 109 mg chol., 1,118 mg sodium, 30 g carbo., 3 g fiber, 36 g pro.

PREP: 20 minutes
BAKE: 50 minutes   OVEN: 350°F

8 servings	ingredients	4 servings
8 cups (about 2½ lb.)	chopped cooked chicken	4 cups (about 1¼ lb.)
4 medium	zucchini, halved lengthwise and sliced in ½-inch pieces	2 medium
2 10.75-oz. cans	condensed cream of chicken soup	1 10.75-oz. can
1 cup	chicken broth	½ cup
1 cup	chopped red onion	½ cup
4 cloves	garlic, minced	2 cloves
1 tsp.	Greek seasoning	½ tsp.
six 6-inch	pita bread rounds, torn into bite-size pieces	three 6-inch
2 cups (8 oz.)	crumbled feta cheese	1 cup (4 oz.)
1 cup	pitted kalamata olives, sliced	½ cup
¼ cup	olive oil	2 Tbsp.
4 cups	chopped roma tomatoes	2 cups

Smoked Chicken Strata

Call on strata—the classic brunch dish—for special holiday mornings or for evenings when "breakfast for supper" sounds especially good.

PREP: 25 minutes   CHILL: 2 to 24 hours   BAKE: 25 minutes   STAND: 10 minutes   OVEN: 325°F

6 servings	ingredients	4 servings
1 Tbsp.	vegetable oil	2 tsp.
2 cups	cut-up fresh asparagus or chopped fresh broccoli	1⅓ cups
1½ cups	sliced fresh mushrooms	1 cup
½ cup	chopped red or yellow sweet pepper	⅓ cup
	Nonstick cooking spray	
3	whole grain English muffins, torn or cut into bite-size pieces	2
2 cups (about 10 oz.)	shredded smoked chicken or cooked chicken breast	1⅓ cups (about 7 oz.)
¾ cup (3 oz.)	shredded Swiss cheese	½ cup (2 oz.)
4	eggs, beaten	3
1 cup	milk	⅔
⅛ tsp.	ground black pepper	⅛ tsp.

1 Preheat oven to 325°F. In a large nonstick skillet heat oil over medium-high heat. Add asparagus, mushrooms, and sweet pepper; cook and stir about 3 minutes or just until vegetables are crisp-tender.

2 For 6 servings, lightly coat six 12-ounce casseroles with cooking spray. Divide half the English muffin pieces among the dishes. Top with chicken, asparagus mixture, and two-thirds of the cheese. Top with the remaining English muffin pieces.

3 In a bowl whisk together eggs, milk, and black pepper. Evenly pour egg mixture over the layers in dishes. Using the back of a large spoon, press down muffin pieces to moisten. Sprinkle with the remaining cheese. Cover and refrigerate for 2 to 24 hours.

4 Bake, uncovered, for 25 to 30 minutes or until a knife inserted in centers comes out clean. Let stand for 10 minutes before serving.

For 4 servings: Prepare using method above, except assemble and bake in four 12-ounce casseroles.

PER SERVING: 277 cal., 12 g total fat (4 g sat. fat), 178 mg chol., 746 mg sodium, 21 g carbo., 4 g fiber, 23 g pro.

Chicken Alfredo and Rice Casserole

To prepare two cups of soft bread crumbs, tear three to four slices of day-old bread in small pieces. Place in a food processor or blender and pulse until light, fluffy crumbs form.

1 Preheat oven to 350°F. In a large bowl combine pasta sauce and milk. Stir in rice, chicken, peas, roasted red peppers, almonds (if using), and basil. For 8 servings, transfer to a 3-quart casserole. Cover with foil.

2 Bake for 30 minutes. Uncover and stir. In a bowl combine bread crumbs and melted butter; sprinkle on pasta mixture. Bake, uncovered, for 20 to 25 minutes more or until heated through and crumbs are golden. Let stand for 5 minutes before serving.

For 4 servings: Prepare using method above, except bake in a 1½-quart casserole.

PER SERVING: 456 cal., 16 g total fat (8 g sat. fat), 97 mg chol., 672 mg sodium, 45 g carbo., 3 g fiber, 32 g pro.

PREP: 25 minutes   BAKE: 50 minutes
STAND: 5 minutes   OVEN: 350°F

8 servings	ingredients	4 servings
2 10-oz. containers	refrigerated light Alfredo pasta sauce	1 10-oz. container
1 cup	milk	½ cup
5 cups	cooked white rice or wild rice	2½ cups
4 cups (about 1¼ lb.)	cubed cooked chicken	2 cups (about 10 oz.)
2 cups	frozen peas	1 cup
⅔ cup	chopped bottled roasted red sweet peppers	⅓ cup
½ cup	slivered almonds, toasted (optional)	¼ cup
2 Tbsp.	snipped fresh basil	1 Tbsp.
2 cups	soft bread crumbs	1 cup
2 Tbsp.	butter, melted	1 Tbsp.

Hot and Cheesy Chicken Casserole

Here's what every busy mom is looking for—nearly every food group in one quick-fix dish. To complete the food pyramid, serve this colorful casserole with a spinach-orange salad.

PREP: 35 minutes
BAKE: 35 minutes
OVEN: 350°F

8 servings	ingredients	4 servings
3 cups (about 15 oz.)	chopped cooked chicken	1½ cups (about 8 oz.)
1 14-oz. pkg.	frozen broccoli florets	½ 14-oz. pkg.
1 cup	cooked rice	2 cups
1½ cups	frozen peas	¾ cup
1 10.75-oz. can	condensed cream of chicken soup	½ 10.75-oz. can
1 10.75-oz. can	condensed fiesta nacho cheese soup	½ 10.75-oz. can
1 10-oz. can	diced tomatoes and green chiles, undrained	¾ cup
½ cup	milk	¼ cup
½ tsp.	crushed red pepper (optional)	¼ tsp.
½ cup (2 oz.)	shredded cheddar cheese	¼ cup (1 oz.)
½ cup (2 oz.)	shredded mozzarella cheese	¼ cup (1 oz.)
1 cup	crushed rich round crackers	½ cup

1 Preheat oven to 350°F. For 8 servings, place chicken in a 3-quart rectangular baking dish. In large bowl combine broccoli, rice, and peas. Spread mixture over chicken.

2 In a bowl combine cream of chicken soup, nacho cheese soup, undrained tomatoes and chiles, milk, and, if desired, crushed red pepper. Stir in half the cheddar cheese and half the mozzarella cheese. Pour mixture over broccoli mixture in baking dish. Evenly sprinkle crushed crackers over all. Top with the remaining cheddar and mozzarella cheeses.

3 Bake, uncovered, 35 to 40 minutes or until topping is golden.

For 4 servings: Prepare using method above, except assemble and bake in a 1½-quart gratin dish. If you prefer not to use half cans of soup, omit the condensed cream of chicken soup and use all of the condensed fiesta nacho cheese soup.

PER SERVING: 354 cal., 15 g total fat (6 g sat. fat), 65 mg chol., 886 mg sodium, 29 g carbo., 4 g fiber, 26 g pro.

Lazy Paella

Preparing the Spanish specialty paella [pi-AY-yuh] is normally a long and involved process. This recipe, however, yields scrumptious results with a fraction of the effort.

PREP: 25 minutes   BAKE: 45 minutes
STAND: 10 minutes   OVEN: 350°F

8 servings	ingredients	4 servings
	Nonstick cooking spray	
¼ cup	vegetable oil	2 Tbsp.
5 to 6 lb.	chicken thighs, skinned	2½ to 3 lb.
2 14-oz. cans	chicken broth	1 14-oz. can
2 cups	long grain rice	1 cup
2 cups	frozen peas, thawed	1 cup
2 cups	cooked peeled, and deveined shrimp	1 cup
2 4-oz. cans	(drained weight) sliced mushrooms, drained	1 4-oz. can
¼ cup	dry onion soup mix	2 Tbsp.
	Salt	
	Ground black pepper	
	Paprika	

1 Preheat oven to 350°F. For 8 servings, lightly coat two 3-quart rectangular baking dishes with cooking spray; set aside. In a large skillet heat half the oil over medium heat. Add half the chicken; cook in hot oil, turning to brown evenly. Remove chicken from skillet; set aside. Repeat with remaining chicken and oil.

2 In a large bowl combine broth, uncooked rice, peas, shrimp, mushrooms, and dry soup mix. Divide mixture between prepared baking dishes. Arrange chicken on rice mixture. Lightly sprinkle chicken with salt, pepper, and paprika. Tightly cover baking dishes with foil.

3 Bake about 45 minutes or until chicken is no longer pink (180°F). Let stand, covered, for 10 minutes before serving.

For 4 servings: Prepare using method above, except assemble and bake in one 3-quart rectangular baking dish and in Step 1, brown chicken all at once.

PER SERVING: 500 cal., 12 g total fat (2 g sat. fat), 212 mg chol., 1,101 mg sodium, 47 g carbo., 3 g fiber, 49 g pro.

Spicy Chicken-and-Rice Bake

Invite healthful black beans to the table. These velvet-texture black beauties are inexpensive, rich in cholesterol-reducing fiber, and packed with disease-fighting antioxidants.

1 Preheat oven to 375°F. In a large saucepan heat oil over medium heat. Add onion, sweet pepper, and garlic; cook and stir until vegetables are tender. Stir in beans, undrained tomatoes, tomato juice, corn, uncooked rice, chili powder, salt, and cayenne pepper. Bring to boiling. For 12 servings, divide rice mixture between two 3-quart rectangular baking dishes.

2 Arrange chicken pieces on the rice mixture. Lightly sprinkle chicken with salt, black pepper, and paprika. Tightly cover baking dishes tightly with foil.

3 Bake for 55 to 60 minutes or until chicken is no longer pink (170°F for breasts; 180°F for thighs and drumsticks) and rice is tender.

For 6 servings: Prepare using method above, except assemble and bake in one 3-quart rectangular baking dish.

PER SERVING: 446 cal., 15 g total fat (4 g sat. fat), 104 mg chol., 854 mg sodium, 39 g carbo., 6 g fiber, 40 g pro.

PREP: 25 minutes
BAKE: 55 minutes   OVEN: 375°F

12 servings	ingredients	6 servings
2 Tbsp.	vegetable oil	1 Tbsp.
1 cup	chopped onion	½ cup
1 cup	chopped green sweet pepper	½ cup
4 cloves	garlic, minced	2 cloves
2 15-oz. cans	black beans, rinsed and drained	1 15-oz. can
2 14.5-oz. cans	diced tomatoes, undrained	1 14.5-oz. can
2 cups	tomato juice	1 cup
2 cups	frozen whole kernel corn	1 cup
1⅓ cups	long grain rice	⅔ cup
2 tsp.	chili powder	1 tsp.
1 tsp.	salt	½ tsp.
¼ to ½ tsp.	cayenne pepper	⅛ to ¼ tsp.
6 lb.	meaty chicken pieces (small breast halves, thighs, and drumsticks), skinned	3 lb.
	Salt	
	Black pepper	
	Paprika	

Chicken and Noodles with Vegetables

Warm, tender, and fragrant, this dish is the quintessential comfort food to bring the family to the table on a chilly winter evening.

PREP: 30 minutes
COOK: 8 to 9 hours (low)
or 4 to 4½ hours (high)

9 servings	ingredients	6 servings
3 cups	sliced carrots	2 cups
2¼ cups	chopped onions	1½ cups
1½ cups	sliced celery	1 cup
1	bay leaf	1
6 medium (about 3¾ lb. total)	chicken legs (drumstick-thigh portion), skinned	4 medium (about 2½ lb. total)
3 10.75-oz. cans	reduced-fat and reduced-sodium condensed cream of chicken soup	2 10.75-oz. cans
¾ cup	water	½ cup
1½ tsp.	salt	1 tsp.
1½ tsp.	dried thyme, crushed	1 tsp.
¼ teaspoon	ground black pepper	¼ tsp.
6 cups (12 oz.)	dried wide noodles	4 cups (8 oz.)
1½ cups	frozen peas	1 cup

1 For 9 servings, in a 5- to 6-quart slow cooker stir together carrots, onions, celery, and bay leaf. Place chicken on vegetables. In a large bowl stir together soup, the water, salt, thyme, and pepper. Pour over chicken in cooker. Cover and cook on low-heat setting for 8 to 9 hours or on high-heat setting for 4 to 4½ hours.

2 To serve, cook noodles according to package directions. Drain; return to pan. Cover and keep warm. Remove chicken from slow cooker; cool slightly. Discard bay leaf. Stir frozen peas into mixture in slow cooker. Remove and discard bones from chicken. Shred or chop chicken; stir into mixture in slow cooker.

3 In a large serving bowl combine chicken mixture and noodles.

For 6 servings: Prepare using method above, except use a 3½- or 4-quart slow cooker.

PER SERVING: 288 cal., 5 g total fat (2 g sat. fat), 69 mg chol., 680 mg sodium, 44 g carbo., 5 g fiber, 17 g pro.

Chicken and Orzo Casserole

Smoked paprika—a strikingly red, super-aromatic powder—is made by smoking Spanish pimiento peppers over an oak fire. It's more expensive than ordinary paprika, but once you experience its deep flavor, you'll have no other.

PREP: 15 minutes   BAKE: 20 minutes
STAND: 10 minutes   OVEN: 350°F

8 servings	ingredients	4 servings
4 tsp.	cumin seeds	2 tsp.
2 14.5-oz. cans	stewed tomatoes, undrained	1 14.5-oz. can
2 14-oz. cans	chicken broth	1 14-oz. can
2 cups (12 oz.)	dried orzo pasta	1 cup (6 oz.)
½ cup	oil-packed dried tomatoes, cut up	¼ cup
4 9-oz. pkg.	southwest-flavor frozen cooked chicken breast strips, thawed	2 9-oz. pkg.
	Smoked paprika (optional)	
	Seeded and chopped jalapeño chile peppers (optional)*	

1 Preheat oven to 350°F. In a large saucepan heat cumin seeds over medium heat for 3 to 4 minutes or until seeds are toasted and aromatic, shaking pan occasionally. Carefully stir in undrained tomatoes, broth, orzo, and tomatoes. Bring to boiling. For 8 servings, divide mixture between two 2-quart casseroles. Top with chicken strips. Cover casseroles.

2 Bake for 20 minutes or until orzo is tender. Let stand, covered, for 10 minutes before serving. If desired, top with paprika and jalapeño peppers.

For 4 servings: Prepare using method above, except bake in one 2-quart casserole.

PER SERVING: 388 cal., 7 g total fat (2 g sat. fat), 60 mg chol., 1,227 mg sodium, 44 g carbo., 3 g fiber, 35 g pro.

***Note:** Because hot chile peppers such as jalapeños contain volatile oils that can burn your skin and eyes, avoid direct contact with them as much as possible. When wrking with chile peppers, wear plastic or rubber gloves. If your bare hands do touch the chile peppers, wash your hands well with soap and water.

Chicken Caesar Lasagna

Serve this delicious dish to introduce your family to healthful, fiber-rich whole wheat pasta.

1 Preheat oven to 325°F. Cook noodles according to package directions. Drain; rinse with cold water; drain again. Meanwhile, in a bowl combine Alfredo sauce, lemon juice, and black pepper. Stir in chicken, spinach, and roasted red peppers.

2 For 9 servings, lightly coat a 3-quart rectangular baking dish with cooking spray. Arrange one-third of the noodles in bottom of dish. Top with one-third of the chicken mixture. Repeat layers twice. Cover with foil.

3 Bake for 45 to 55 minutes or until heated through. Uncover; sprinkle with cheese. Bake, uncovered, for 5 minutes more or until cheese is melted. Let stand for 15 minutes before serving.

For 6 servings: Prepare as above, except assemble and bake in a 2-quart rectangular baking dish.

PER SERVING: 268 cal., 10 g total fat (6 g sat. fat), 68 mg chol., 557 mg sodium, 20 g carbo., 2 g fiber, 24 g pro.

PREP: 35 minutes   BAKE: 50 minutes
STAND: 15 minutes   OVEN: 325°F

9 servings	ingredients	6 servings
9	dried whole wheat or regular lasagna noodles	6
2 10-oz. containers	refrigerated light Alfredo pasta sauce	1 10-oz. container
3 Tbsp.	lemon juice	2 Tbsp.
½ tsp.	cracked black pepper	¼ tsp.
3 cups (about 15 oz.)	chopped cooked chicken breast	2 cups (about 10 oz.)
1 10-oz. pkg.	frozen chopped spinach, thawed and well drained	½ 10-oz. pkg.
1 cup	chopped bottled roasted red sweet peppers	⅔ cup
	Nonstick cooking spray	
¾ cup (3 oz.)	shredded Italian-blend cheese	½ cup (2 oz.)

Herbed Chicken and Orzo

Most casseroles are weeknight family fare. Others rise to any occasion, special enough to serve to company. This luxurious concoction is one of them. Choose it when you have guests to impress.

1 Preheat oven to 350°F. For 12 servings, grease two 3-quart oval or rectangular baking dishes; set aside.

2 Cook orzo according to package directions, adding green beans during last 3 minutes of cooking; drain. Meanwhile, cut each chicken in 6 pieces; set aside.

3 In a large bowl whisk together cheese and milk until combined. Add hot orzo mixture; stir until coated. Stir in shredded carrots. Spoon into prepared baking dishes. Top with chicken pieces.

4 Bake, covered, for 30 to 40 minutes or until heated through. Let stand 5 minutes. Sprinkle with parsley.

For 6 servings: Prepare using the method above, except bake in one 3-quart oval or rectangular baking dish.

PER SERVING: 529 cal., 34 g total fat (19 g sat. fat), 159 mg chol., 1,522 mg sodium, 20 g carbo., 0 g fiber, 35 g pro.

PREP: 30 minutes   BAKE: 30 minutes
STAND: 5 minutes   OVEN: 350°F

12 servings	ingredients	6 servings
1 lb.	dried orzo	8 oz.
3 cups (12 oz.)	1-inch pieces fresh green beans	1½ cups (6 oz.)
2	whole roasted deli chicken(s)	1
4 5.2 oz. containers	semisoft cheese with garlic and herbs	2 5.2 oz. containers
1 cup	milk	½ cup
3 cups	shredded carrots	1½ cups
¼ cup	snipped fresh Italian (flat-leaf) parsley	2 Tbsp.

Florentine Chicken-Artichoke Bake

Frozen spinach holds a lot of liquid. To make sure that it is adequately drained, use the heel of your hand to firmly press spinach against the side of a colander until all liquid is released.

PREP: 30 minutes
BAKE: 30 minutes   OVEN: 350°F

12 servings	ingredients	6 servings
7 cups (16 oz.)	dried bow tie or rotini pasta	3½ cups (8 oz.)
¼ cup	butter	2 Tbsp.
⅔ cup	chopped onion	⅓ cup
4	eggs	2
2½ cups	milk	1¼ cups
2 tsp.	dried Italian seasoning, crushed	1 tsp.
1 tsp.	salt	½ tsp.
½ tsp.	ground black pepper	¼ tsp.
4 cups (about 1¼ lb.)	chopped cooked chicken	2 cups (about 10 oz.)
4 cups (16 oz.)	shredded Monterey Jack cheese	2 cups (8 oz.)
2 14-oz. cans	artichoke hearts, drained and quartered	1 14-oz. can
2 10-oz. pkg.	frozen chopped spinach, thawed and well drained	1 10-oz. pkg.
1 cup	oil-packed dried tomatoes, drained and chopped	½ cup
½ cup	grated Parmesan cheese	¼ cup
1 cup	soft bread crumbs	½ cup
1 tsp.	paprika	½ tsp.

1 Preheat oven to 350°F. Cook pasta according to package directions. Drain; set aside. Meanwhile, in a large skillet melt half the butter over medium heat. Add onion; cook and stir in hot butter about 5 minutes or until tender. Remove from heat; set aside.

2 In an extra-large bowl whisk together eggs, milk, Italian seasoning, salt, and pepper. Stir in chicken, Monterey Jack cheese, artichoke hearts, spinach, tomatoes, and half the Parmesan cheese. Toss with cooked pasta and cooked onion mixture. For 12 servings, divide mixture between two 3-quart rectangular baking dishes. Cover with foil.

3 Bake for 20 minutes. Meanwhile, in a small saucepan melt remaining butter; remove from heat. Stir in the remaining Parmesan cheese, bread crumbs, and paprika. Sprinkle crumb mixture over pasta. Bake, uncovered, for 10 minutes more or until heated through.

For 6 servings: Prepare using method above, except bake in one 3-quart rectangular baking dish.

PER SERVING: 531 cal., 24 g total fat (13 g sat. fat), 163 mg chol., 897 mg sodium, 41 g carbo., 5 g fiber, 36 g pro.

Chicken Supreme Casserole

Mayonnaise is the ingredient that makes the sauce silky and the flavor unforgettable.

1 Preheat oven to 350°F. Cook pasta according to package directions, adding the stir-fry vegetables the last 5 minutes of cooking; drain well.

2 Meanwhile, in a large bowl stir together the soup, milk, mayonnaise, and pepper. Stir in cooked pasta mixture and chicken.

3 For 6 servings, transfer pasta mixture to a 3-quart rectangular baking dish. In a bowl toss together bread cubes, melted butter, and garlic powder; sprinkle over pasta mixture.

4 Bake, uncovered, for 30 to 35 minutes or until heated through and bread cubes are golden. Let stand for 10 minutes. If desired, sprinkle with parsley.

For 3 servings: Prepare using method above, except assemble and bake in a 1½-quart gratin dish.

PER SERVING: 584 cal., 25 g total fat (8 g sat. fat), 71 mg chol., 1,123 mg sodium, 60 g carbo., 4 g fiber, 28 g pro.

PREP: 25 minutes BAKE: 30 minutes
STAND: 10 minutes OVEN: 350°F

6 servings	ingredients	3 servings
3¼ cups (8 oz.)	dried farfalle (bow tie) pasta	1⅔ cups (4 oz.)
1 16-oz. pkg.	frozen stir-fry vegetables (broccoli, carrots, onions, red peppers, celery, water chestnuts, and mushrooms)	½ 16-oz. pkg.
2 10.75-oz. cans	condensed cream of chicken soup	1 10.75-oz. can
2 cups	milk	1 cup
¼ cup	mayonnaise or salad dressing	2 Tbsp.
¼ tsp.	ground black pepper	⅛ tsp.
2 cups (about 10 oz.)	chopped cooked chicken	1 cup (about 5 oz.)
2 cups	French bread cubes	1 cup
2 Tbsp.	butter or margarine, melted	1 Tbsp.
¼ tsp.	garlic powder	⅛ tsp.
1 Tbsp.	snipped fresh parsley (optional)	2 tsp.

Potluck Chicken Tetrazzini

This classic casserole was created in honor of the Italian opera singer Louisa Tetrazzini. One bite of its glorious richness will have taste buds singing.

PREP: 30 minutes
BAKE: 15 minutes
STAND: 5 minutes
OVEN: 350°F

10 servings	ingredients	5 servings
8 oz.	dried spaghetti or linguine, broken in half	4 oz.
12 oz.	fresh asparagus, trimmed and cut in 1-inch pieces	6 oz.
2 Tbsp.	butter	1 Tbsp.
8 oz.	small whole fresh mushrooms*	4 oz.
3 medium	red and/or yellow sweet peppers, seeded and cut in 1-inch pieces	1½ medium
¼ cup	all-purpose flour	2 Tbsp.
⅛ tsp.	ground black pepper	⅛ tsp.
1 14-oz. can	chicken broth	1 cup
¾ cup	milk	⅓ cup
3 cups (about 15 oz.)	chopped cooked chicken	1½ cups (about 8 oz.)
½ cup (2 oz.)	shredded Swiss cheese	¼ cup (1 oz.)
1 Tbsp.	finely shredded lemon peel	2½ tsp.
1½ cups	sourdough bread cubes	¾ cup
1 Tbsp.	olive oil	2½ tsp.
2 Tbsp.	snipped fresh parsley (optional)	1 Tbsp.

1 Preheat oven to 350°F. Cook spaghetti according to package directions, adding the asparagus the last 1 minute of cooking. Drain; return to pan. Set aside.

2 Meanwhile, in large skillet melt butter over medium heat. Add mushrooms and sweet peppers; cook and stir in hot butter for 8 to 10 minutes or until mushrooms are tender. Stir in flour and black pepper. Add broth and milk. Cook and stir until thickened and bubbly.

3 Add mushroom mixture, chicken, cheese, and half the lemon peel to pasta; toss gently to coat. For 10 servings, transfer pasta mixture to a 3-quart rectangular baking dish.

4 In a bowl toss together bread cubes, oil, and the remaining lemon peel. Sprinkle bread cube mixture over pasta mixture.

5 Bake, uncovered, for 15 minutes or until heated through. Let stand for 5 minutes. If desired, sprinkle with parsley.

For 5 servings: Prepare using the method above, except assemble and bake in a 1½-quart gratin dish.

*Note: If mushrooms are large, cut them in half quarters, then in pieces about 1- to 1½-inches.

PER SERVING: 282 cal., 10 g total fat (4 g sat. fat), 48 mg chol., 258 mg sodium, 28 g carbo., 2 g fiber, 20 g pro.

Lemon Chicken Pasta Toss

A bit more work, but worth the effort—freshly squeezed lemon juice tastes much more alive than bottled versions. The juice adds zesty flavor to this quick-to-make dish.

PREP: 20 minutes
COOK: 20 minutes

4 servings	ingredients	2 servings
2 cups (6 oz.)	dried multigrain penne pasta	1 cup (3 oz.)
12 oz.	skinless, boneless chicken breasts, cut in 1-inch pieces	6 oz.
2 Tbsp.	all-purpose flour	1 Tbsp.
2 Tbsp.	olive oil	1 Tbsp.
1/3 cup	finely chopped shallot	3 Tbsp.
2 cloves	garlic, minced	1 clove
3/4 cup	chicken broth	1/2 cup
3 Tbsp.	freshly squeezed lemon juice	4 1/2 tsp.
1/4 tsp.	salt	1/8 tsp.
1/4 tsp.	ground black pepper	1/8 tsp.
1 cup	halved yellow and/or cherry tomatoes	1/2 cup
3 Tbsp.	capers, drained	2 Tbsp.
3 Tbsp.	snipped Italian (flat-leaf) parsley	2 Tbsp.
	Freshly grated Parmesan cheese (optional)	

1 Cook pasta according to package directions. Drain; return pasta to hot pan. Cover and keep warm.

2 Meanwhile, in a bowl toss together chicken and flour until chicken is lightly coated. In a large skillet heat half the oil over medium-high heat. Add chicken; cook and stir for 6 to 8 minutes or until chicken is no longer pink. Remove chicken from skillet; set aside.

3 Reduce heat to medium. Add the remaining oil to skillet. Add shallot and garlic; cook and stir for 1 minute or until tender. Carefully stir in broth, lemon juice, salt, and pepper. For 4 servings, cook, uncovered, for 2 to 3 minutes or until reduced to about 2/3 cup. Stir in chicken, tomatoes, capers, and parsley; heat through.

4 Toss pasta with chicken mixture. If desired, serve with cheese.

For 2 servings: Prepare using method above, except in Step 3 reduce mixture to 1/3 cup.

PER SERVING: 339 cal., 9 g total fat (1 g sat. fat), 50 mg chol., 589 mg sodium, 36 g carbo., 4 g fiber, 29 g pro.

Mediterranean Chicken and Pasta

Campanelle (kah-pah-NELL-eh) means "little bell" in Italian. The pasta has an open-vessel shape that holds the piquant artichoke marinade.

1 Drain artichokes, reserving marinade. Set aside. For 8 servings, in an extra-large skillet heat half the oil over medium-high heat. Add half the chicken and half the garlic; cook and stir until chicken is browned. Using a slotted spoon, remove chicken and garlic from skillet; set aside. Repeat with remaining oil, chicken, and garlic. Return all the chicken and garlic to the skillet. Add the reserved artichoke marinade, broth, and wine.

2 Bring to boiling; reduce heat. Simmer, covered, for 10 minutes. Stir in artichokes, roasted red pepper strips, olives, and oregano. Heat through.

3 Serve the chicken mixture over hot cooked pasta. If desired, sprinkle with cheese.

For 4 servings: Prepare using method above; except in Step 1 use a large skillet and brown chicken all at once.

PER SERVING: 337 cal., 9 g total fat (1 g sat. fat), 49 mg chol., 323 mg sodium, 36 g carbo., 2 g fiber, 26 g pro.

START TO FINISH: 30 minutes

8 servings	ingredients	4 servings
2 6-oz. jars	marinated artichoke hearts	1 6-oz. jar
2 Tbsp.	olive oil	1 Tbsp.
1½ lb.	skinless, boneless chicken breast halves, cut in ¾-inch cubes	12 oz.
6 cloves	garlic, thinly sliced	3 cloves
½ cup	chicken broth	¼ cup
½ cup	dry white wine	¼ cup
2 7-oz. jars	roasted red sweet peppers, drained and cut in strips	1 7-oz. jar
½ cup	pitted kalamata olives	¼ cup
2 Tbsp.	snipped fresh oregano	1 Tbsp.
6 cups	hot cooked campanelle or penne pasta	3 cups
½ cup (2 oz.)	crumbled feta cheese (optional)	¼ cup (1 oz.)

Chicken Fajita Pasta

Even the fussiest young eaters warm to foods flavored with Mexican spices. This kid-friendly recipe will be a popular request.

1 Cook pasta according to package directions. Drain and return pasta to pan. Cover and keep warm. Meanwhile, in a bowl combine sour cream, marinade, lime juice, chili powder, cumin, and crushed red pepper. Set aside.

2 In a large skillet heat half the oil over medium heat. Add onion, sweet pepper, and Anaheim pepper; cook and stir for 4 to 5 minutes or until crisp-tender. Remove vegetables from skillet; set aside.

3 Add remaining oil to skillet. Turn heat to medium-high. Add half the chicken; cook and stir for 2 to 3 minutes or until chicken is no longer pink. Remove chicken from skillet; set aside. Repeat with remaining chicken (if necessary, add additional oil).

4 Add all the chicken, the vegetables, and sour cream mixture to pasta. Toss to coat. Heat through over low heat. If desired, sprinkle with cilantro and serve with lime wedges.

PER SERVING: 453 cal., 15 g total fat (6 g sat. fat), 60 mg chol., 589 mg sodium, 53 g carbo., 3 g fiber, 27 g pro.

START TO FINISH: 35 minutes

6 servings	ingredients	4 servings
12 oz.	dried pappardelle pasta or egg noodles	8 oz.
1 8-oz. carton	sour cream	2/3 cup
1/2 cup	chipotle-flavor liquid meat marinade	1/3 cup
2 Tbsp.	lime juice	4 tsp.
1 tsp.	chili powder	3/4 tsp.
1 tsp.	ground cumin	3/4 tsp.
1/2 tsp.	crushed red pepper	1/4 tsp.
2 Tbsp.	olive oil	4 tsp.
1 medium	onion, halved and thinly sliced	1 small
1 medium	red sweet pepper, cut in thin bite-size strips	1 small
1	fresh Anaheim chile pepper, seeded and cut into thin bite-size strips (see note, page 52)	1/2
3 large (1 to 1 1/4 lb. total)	skinless, boneless chicken breast halves, cut in thin bite-size strips	2 large (11 to 13 oz. total)
1 Tbsp.	snipped fresh cilantro (optional)	2 tsp.
	Lime wedges (optional)	

Creamy Ranch Chicken

When your objective is making eaters absolutely ecstatic, remember these four words: Bring. On. The. Bacon.

START TO FINISH: 30 minutes

8 servings	ingredients	4 servings
6 cups (12 oz.)	dried medium noodles	3 cups (6 oz.)
12 slices	bacon, cut in narrow strips	6 slices
8 medium (2 to 2½ lb. total)	boneless chicken breast halves, cut in bite-size pieces	4 medium (1 to 1¼ lb. total)
¼ cup	all-purpose flour	2 Tbsp.
¼ cup	ranch dry salad dressing mix	2 Tbsp.
2½ cups	whole milk	1¼ cups
2 Tbsp.	finely shredded Parmesan cheese	1 Tbsp.

1 Cook noodles according to package directions. Drain; return to pan. Cover and keep warm.

2 For 8 servings, in an extra-large skillet cook bacon over medium heat until crisp. Drain bacon on paper towels; discard all but ¼ cup drippings.

3 In the same skillet cook and stir half the chicken in reserved drippings until tender and no longer pink. Using a slotted spoon, remove chicken from skillet; set aside. Repeat with remaining chicken. Return all chicken to the skillet.

4 Sprinkle flour and salad dressing mix on the chicken; stir well. Stir in milk. Cook and stir until thickened and bubbly. Cook and stir for 1 minute more. Stir in bacon.

5 Serve chicken mixture with noodles; sprinkle with cheese.

For 4 servings: Prepare using method above, except use a large skillet and in Step 2 reserve 2 tablespoons drippings in skillet. In Step 3 cook all of the chicken at once.

PER SERVING: 488 cal., 18 g total fat (7 g sat. fat), 137 mg chol., 574 mg sodium, 27 g carbo., 1 g fiber, 45 g pro.

Italian Chicken and Pasta

Thighs are the most succulent, flavorful part of the chicken. Unlike breasts, which become dry in a slow cooker, thighs remain moist and tender when cooked slowly for hours.

1 For 4 servings, in 3½- or 4-quart slow cooker combine beans, onion, and mushrooms. Place chicken on vegetables. In a small bowl combine tomato sauce and Italian seasoning. Pour over chicken.

2 Cover and cook on low-heat setting for 5 to 6 hours or high-heat setting for 2½ to 3 hours.

3 Stir in chopped tomato. Serve chicken mixture over hot cooked noodles. If desired, sprinkle with cheese.

For 2 servings: Prepare using method above, except use a 1½-quart slow cooker. If only one heat setting is available, cook for 4 to 5 hours.

PER SERVING: 318 cal., 7 g total fat (2 g sat. fat), 117 mg chol., 614 mg sodium, 33 g carbo., 4 g fiber, 30 g pro.

PREP: 20 minutes   COOK: 5 to 6 hours (low) or 2½ to 3 hours (high)

4 servings	ingredients	2 servings
2 cups	frozen Italian green beans or regular green beans	1 cup
1 medium	onion, cut in ¼-inch slices	1 small
1 cup	fresh mushrooms, quartered	½ cup
1 lb.	skinless, boneless chicken thighs, cut in 1-inch pieces	8 oz.
1 15-oz. can	tomato sauce	1 8-oz. can
1 tsp.	dried Italian seasoning, crushed	½ tsp.
⅔ cup	chopped roma tomato	⅓ cup
2 cups	hot cooked noodles	1 cup
	Finely shredded Parmesan cheese (optional)	

Chicken Scaloppine

If you don't have la meat mallet for pounding the chicken breasts, a rolling pin works as an effective substitute.

1 Place each chicken breast half between two pieces of plastic wrap. Using the flat side of a meat mallet, lightly pound chicken to about ¼-inch thickness. Remove plastic wrap. Sprinkle chicken with salt and pepper.

2 In a shallow dish combine egg(s) and milk. In a second shallow dish combine seasoned bread crumbs and cheese. Dip each chicken piece in flour, then in egg mixture; coat with bread crumb mixture, pressing with your hands until the crumb mixture adheres to the chicken.

3 For 4 servings, in a very large skillet melt butter over medium-high heat; add oil. Add two of the chicken pieces and cook about 8 minutes or until chicken is no longer pink (170°F), turning once halfway through cooking. Remove from skillet; keep warm. If necessary, add additional oil to skillet. Repeat with remaining chicken. If desired, serve with spaghetti, pasta sauce, and Parmesan cheese.

For 2 servings: Prepare using method above, except fry chicken pieces in one batch.

PER SERVING: 523 cal., 23 g total fat (8 g sat. fat), 215 mg chol., 1,442 mg sodium, 29 g carbo., 0 g fiber, 47 g pro.

PREP: 20 minutes
COOK: 8 minutes per batch

4 servings	ingredients	2 servings
4 5-oz.	skinless, boneless chicken breast halves	2 5-oz.
½ tsp.	salt	¼ tsp.
¼ tsp.	ground black pepper	⅛ tsp.
2	egg(s), beaten	1
2 Tbsp.	milk	1 Tbsp.
1 cup	seasoned fine dry bread crumbs	½ cup
¾ cup	finely shredded Romano or Parmesan cheese	½ cup
⅓ cup	all-purpose flour	¼ cup
2 Tbsp.	butter	1 Tbsp.
2 Tbsp.	olive oil	1 Tbsp.
4	lemon wedges	2
	Hot cooked spaghetti (optional)	
	Pasta sauce (optional)	
	Grated Parmesan cheese (optional)	

Cheesy Turkey-and-Spinach Pie

Supermarket packages of fresh herbs usually contain more leaves than you can use in one recipe. To store extra herbs, place herb stems in a glass of water, cover loosely with a plastic bag, and refrigerate.

PREP: 30 minutes
BAKE: 45 minutes
STAND: 10 minutes
OVEN: 350°F

12 servings	ingredients	6 servings
	Nonstick cooking spray	
3¹/₂ cups (8 oz.)	dried fine noodles	1³/₄ cups (4 oz.)
6	eggs, beaten	3
2 8-oz. pkg.	cream cheese or mascarpone cheese, softened	1 8-oz. pkg.
²/₃ cup	sour cream	¹/₃ cup
²/₃ cup	mayonnaise or salad dressing	¹/₃ cup
¹/₂ cup	snipped fresh basil	¹/₄ cup
1 tsp.	garlic salt	¹/₂ tsp.
¹/₂ tsp.	crushed red pepper	¹/₄ tsp.
4 cups (about 1¹/₄ lb.)	chopped cooked turkey	2 cups (about 10 oz.)
2 10-oz. pkg.	frozen chopped spinach, thawed and well drained	1 10-oz. pkg.
2 cups (8 oz.)	shredded Monterey Jack cheese	1 cup (4 oz.)
²/₃ cup	chopped bottled roasted red sweet peppers	¹/₃ cup

1 Preheat oven to 350°F. For 12 servings, coat two 9-inch deep-dish pie plates or two 2-quart square baking dishes with cooking spray; place plates or dishes on baking sheets. Set aside. Cook noodles according to package directions; drain well.

2 Meanwhile, in a large bowl whisk together eggs, cream cheese, sour cream, mayonnaise, basil, garlic salt, and crushed red pepper until well combined. Stir in cooked noodles, turkey, spinach, Monterey Jack cheese, and roasted red peppers. Divide mixture between prepared plates or dishes (pie plates will be very full).

3 Bake, uncovered, for 45 to 50 minutes or until edges are slightly puffed and golden. Let stand for 10 minutes before serving.

For 6 servings: Prepare using method above, except assemble and bake in one 9-inch deep-dish pie plate or one 2-quart square baking dish.

PER SERVING: 520 cal., 37 g total fat (17 g sat. fat), 225 mg chol., 481 mg sodium, 18 g carbo., 3 g fiber, 29 g pro.

Popover Pizza Casserole

Be sure that the ground turkey you purchase for this recipe is 100-percent breast meat. Products labeled "ground turkey" contain a large percentage of unskinned dark meat and may contain excess fat.

PREP: 35 minutes
BAKE: 30 minutes
OVEN: 400°F

6 servings	ingredients	4 servings
1¼ lb.	ground uncooked turkey breast or extra-lean ground beef	12 oz.
2 cups	sliced fresh mushrooms	1⅓ cups
1½ cups	chopped yellow summer squash	1 cup
1 cup	chopped onion	⅔ cup
1 cup	chopped green sweet pepper	⅔ cup
1 14-oz. jar or can	pizza sauce	1 cup
1 tsp.	dried Italian seasoning, crushed	¾ tsp.
½ tsp.	fennel seeds, crushed	¼ tsp.
1 cup	milk	⅔ cup
2	eggs	1 whole and 1 yolk
1 Tbsp.	vegetable oil	2 tsp.
1 cup	all-purpose flour	⅔ cup
1 cup (4 oz.)	mozzarella cheese	⅔ cup (2½ oz.)
2 Tbsp.	grated Parmesan cheese	4 tsp.

1 Preheat oven to 400°F. For 6 servings, in a large oven-going skillet cook turkey, mushrooms, squash, onion, and sweet pepper over medium heat until turkey is browned and vegetables are tender, stirring to break up turkey. Drain off fat. Stir pizza sauce, Italian seasoning, and crushed fennel seeds into turkey mixture. Bring to boiling; reduce heat. Simmer, uncovered, for 5 minutes, stirring occasionally. Spread evenly in skillet.

2 Meanwhile, for topping, in a bowl combine milk, eggs, and oil. Beat with an electric mixer on medium speed or whisk for 1 minute. Add flour; beat or whisk about 1 minute more or until smooth.

3 Sprinkle mozzarella cheese over meat mixture in skillet. Evenly pour topping over mixture, covering completely. Sprinkle with Parmesan cheese.

4 Bake, uncovered, for 30 to 35 minutes or until topping is puffed and golden. (Casserole may look a bit gooey on top of the turkey mixture from the melted cheese.) Serve immediately.

For 4 servings: Prepare using the method above, except use a medium skillet. For eggs, use 1 whole egg and 1 egg yolk instead of 2 whole eggs.

PER SERVING: 360 cal., 11 g total fat (4 g sat. fat), 131 mg chol., 612 mg sodium, 31 g carbo., 3 g fiber, 35 g pro.

Smoked Turkey Jambalaya

Creole flavors—bright and robust—burst from this savory concoction of mixed meats, summer vegetables, and tender white rice.

1 Preheat oven to 350°F. In a saucepan combine water and uncooked rice. Bring to boiling; reduce heat. Cover and simmer for 15 to 18 minutes or until rice is tender and water is absorbed.

2 In a large bowl combine rice, frozen vegetables, undrained tomatoes with green pepper, and undrained tomatoes with green chiles. Stir in kielbasa, green onions, Cajun seasoning, and garlic. Mix well. For 12 servings, divide between two 2-quart square baking dishes.

3 Bake, uncovered, about 55 minutes or until heated through, stirring once. Pass hot pepper sauce.

For 6 servings: Prepare using the method above, except assemble and bake in one 2-quart square baking dish.

PER SERVING: 219 cal., 3 g total fat (0 g sat. fat), 0 mg chol., 842 mg sodium, 35 g carbo., 3 g fiber, 12 g pro.

PREP: 30 minutes
BAKE: 55 minutes
OVEN: 350°F

12 servings	ingredients	6 servings
4 cups	water	2 cups
2 cups	long grain rice	1 cup
2 16-oz. pkg.	frozen peppers and onion stir-fry vegetables	1 16-oz. pkg.
2 14.5-oz. cans	diced tomatoes with green pepper, celery, and onions, undrained	1 14.5-oz. can
2 10-oz. cans	diced tomatoes and green chiles, undrained	1 10-oz. can
1 lb.	turkey kielbasa or other smoked turkey sausage, cut in 1/4-inch rounds	8 oz.
1 cup	sliced green onions	1/2 cup
1 tsp.	Cajun seasoning	1/2 tsp.
2 cloves	garlic, minced	1 clove
	Bottled hot pepper sauce	

One-Dish Turkey and Biscuits

The ideal recipe for the day after Thanksgiving, this quick-fix casserole turns leftover turkey into a delicious treat.

PREP: 30 minutes
BAKE: 20 minutes
OVEN: 425°F

6 servings	ingredients	4 servings
1¹/₃ cups	chicken broth	1 cup
³/₄ cup	finely chopped onion	¹/₂ cup
²/₃ cup	finely chopped celery	¹/₂ cup
2 cups	frozen peas and carrots	1¹/₂ cups
1¹/₃ cups	milk	1 cup
¹/₄ cup	all-purpose flour	3 Tbsp.
2²/₃ cups (about 13 oz.)	cubed cooked turkey breast	2 cups (about 10 oz.)
³/₄ tsp.	dried sage, crushed	¹/₂ tsp.
¹/₈ tsp.	ground black pepper	¹/₈ tsp.
1²/₃ cups	packaged biscuit mix	1¹/₄ cups
²/₃ cup	milk	¹/₂ cup
1 Tbsp.	dried parsley flakes, crushed	2 tsp.

1 Preheat oven to 425°F. In a saucepan combine broth, onion, and celery. Bring to boiling; reduce heat. Cover and simmer for 5 minutes. Add peas and carrots; return to boiling.

2 For 6 servings, in a bowl stir the 1¹/₃ cups milk into flour until well mixed; stir into vegetable mixture in saucepan. Cook and stir until thickened and bubbly. Stir in turkey, sage, and pepper. Transfer to a 3-quart casserole.

3 In a bowl combine biscuit mix, the ²/₃ cup milk, and parsley flakes. Stir with a fork just until moistened. Spoon in 12 mounds on the hot turkey mixture.

4 Bake, uncovered, for 20 to 25 minutes or until biscuits are golden.

For 4 servings: Prepare using method above, except assemble and bake in a 2-quart casserole. In Step 2 use 1 cup milk. In Step 3 use ¹/₂ cup milk and form biscuit dough in 8 mounds.

PER SERVING: 356 cal., 8 g total fat (3 g sat. fat), 67 mg chol., 844 mg sodium, 41 g carbo., 3 g fiber, 30 g pro.

HOMETOWN FAVORITES

Chapter

3

FAMILY-APPROVED MEAT DISHES

RECIPE FINDER

FOR MORE RECIPES:
Visit BHG.com/Recipes

p. 80   p. 90

p. 94   p. 101

p. 103   p. 114

76

Chili-Pasta Skillet, p. 83

Cheeseburger and Fries Casserole

If kids were in charge of family nutrition, this easy-going recipe would be on the menu every night of the week.

PREP: 20 minutes
BAKE: 45 minutes
OVEN: 350°F

16 servings	ingredients	8 servings
4 lb.	lean ground beef	2 lb.
2 10.75-oz. cans	condensed golden mushroom soup	1 10.75-oz. can
2 10.75-oz. cans	condensed cheddar cheese soup	1 10.75-oz. can
2 20-oz. pkg.	frozen french-fried crinkle-cut potatoes	1 20-oz. pkg.
	Toppings (such as ketchup, pickles, mustard, and chopped tomato) (optional)	

1 Preheat oven to 350°F. For 16 servings, in an extra-large skillet cook half of the ground beef until brown, stirring to break up meat. Drain off fat; spoon meat into a 3-quart rectangular baking dish. Repeat with remaining ground beef, using another 3-quart rectangular baking dish. In a bowl combine golden mushroom soup and cheddar cheese soup. Spread over the meat. Layer the potatoes on the soup.

2 Bake, uncovered, for 45 to 55 minutes or until the potatoes are golden. If desired, serve with toppings.

For 8 servings: Prepare using method above, except use a large skillet. Assemble and bake in one 3-quart rectangular baking dish.

PER SERVING: 348 cal., 18 g total fat (6 g sat. fat), 78 mg chol., 654 mg sodium, 24 g carbo., 2 g fiber, 24 g pro.

Hamburger Pie

This hearty casserole has been a family favorite for decades.

PREP: 30 minutes
BAKE: 30 minutes
OVEN: 350°F

12 servings	ingredients	6 servings
2½ lb.	lean ground beef	1¼ lb.
1 cup	chopped onion	½ cup
½ tsp.	salt	¼ tsp.
Several dashes	ground black pepper	Dash
5 cups	frozen cut green beans, thawed	2½ cups
2 10.75-oz. cans	condensed tomato soup	1 10.75-oz. can
2 24-oz. pkg.	refrigerated mashed potatoes	1 24-oz. pkg.
1 cup (4 oz.)	shredded process American cheese	½ cup (2 oz.)

1 Preheat oven to 350°F. For 12 servings, grease two 2-quart rectangular baking dishes; set aside. In an extra-large skillet cook beef and onion until meat is browned and onion is tender, stirring to break up meat. Drain off fat. Add the salt and pepper. Stir in beans and soup. Divide mixture between prepared baking dishes.

2 Spoon potatoes in mounds on the bean mixture (or, if desired, pipe potatoes using a pastry bag and a large star tip). Sprinkle cheese on the potatoes.

3 Bake, uncovered, for 30 to 35 minutes or until mixture is bubbly and cheese begins to brown.

For 6 servings: Prepare using method above, except use a large skillet and assemble and bake in one 2-quart rectangular baking dish.

PER SERVING: 376 cal., 16 g total fat (8 g sat. fat), 80 mg chol., 796 mg sodium, 34 g carbo., 4 g fiber, 23 g pro.

Grandma's Spaghetti Casserole

This old-fashioned supper dish is what Grandma would serve. It's welcoming, warm, and wonderful.

PREP: 35 minutes BAKE: 45 minutes
OVEN: 350°F

8 servings	ingredients	4 servings
16 oz.	dried spaghetti	8 oz.
1 lb.	ground beef	8 oz.
1 cup	chopped onion	½ cup
1 cup	chopped green sweet pepper	½ cup
2 14.5-oz. cans	diced tomatoes, undrained	1 14.5-oz. can
2 10.75-oz. cans	condensed tomato soup	1 10.75-oz. can
1 tsp.	ground black pepper	½ tsp.
4 cups (16 oz.)	shredded cheddar cheese	2 cups (8 oz.)
8 slices	bacon, crisp-cooked, drained, and crumbled	4 slices

1 Preheat oven to 350°F. Cook spaghetti according to package directions; drain. Set aside. For 8 servings, grease two 2-quart casseroles.

2 Meanwhile, in an extra-large skillet cook ground beef, onion, and sweet pepper over medium heat until meat is browned, stirring to break up meat; drain off fat. Stir in undrained tomatoes, soup, and black pepper. Bring just to boiling. Add half the shredded cheese, stirring until melted.

3 Toss meat mixture and bacon with cooked spaghetti. Divide mixture between prepared casseroles. Cover casseroles.

4 Bake for 30 minutes. Uncover; sprinkle with the remaining cheese. Bake, uncovered, about 15 minutes more or until bubbly and heated through.

For 4 servings: Prepare using method above, except use a large skillet and bake in one 2-quart casserole.

PER SERVING: 675 cal., 31 g total fat (16 g sat. fat), 100 mg chol., 1,007 mg sodium, 61 g carbo., 3 g fiber, 35 g pro.

Chili-Pasta Skillet

In this recipe the macaroni cooks along with the other ingredients, saving busy cooks the time and trouble of precooking and draining the pasta.

1 For 12 servings, in an extra-large skillet cook beef and onion until meat is browned and onion is tender, stirring to break up meat. Drain off fat.

2 Stir in beans, undrained tomatoes, tomato sauce, chile peppers, uncooked macaroni, chili powder, and garlic salt. Bring to boiling; reduce heat. Simmer, covered, about 20 minutes or until macaroni is tender, stirring often. Remove skillet from heat; sprinkle mixture with cheese. Cover and let stand about 2 minutes or until cheese is melted.

For 6 servings: Prepare using method above, except use a large skillet.

PER SERVING: 311 cal., 13 g total fat (5 g sat. fat), 56 mg chol., 634 mg sodium, 27 g carbo., 5 g fiber, 24 g pro.

PREP: 15 minutes   COOK: 20 minutes
STAND: 2 minutes

12 servings	ingredients	6 servings
2 lb.	ground beef	1 lb.
1 1/2 cups	chopped onion	3/4 cup
2 15.5-oz. cans	red kidney beans, rinsed and drained	1 15.5-oz. can
2 14.5-oz. cans	diced tomatoes, undrained	1 14.5-oz. can
1 15-oz. can	tomato sauce	1 8-oz. can
2 4-oz. cans	diced green chile peppers, drained	1 4-oz. can
1 cup (4 oz.)	dried elbow macaroni	1/2 cup (2 oz.)
4 to 6 tsp.	chili powder	2 to 3 tsp.
1 tsp.	garlic salt	1/2 tsp.
1 cup (4 oz.)	shredded Monterey Jack cheese or cheddar cheese	1/2 cup (2 oz.)

Mexicali Hamburger Casserole

Spoon into this colorful casserole for a full-fledged fiesta baked beneath a tender crust of corn bread.

PREP: 30 minutes   BAKE: 30 minutes
STAND: 5 minutes   OVEN: 350°F

12 servings	ingredients	6 servings
3 lb.	lean ground beef	1½ lb.
2 14.5-oz. cans	diced tomatoes with chili spices, undrained	1 14.5-oz. can
3 cups	frozen whole kernel corn, thawed	1½ cups
1¼ cups	finely shredded Mexican cheese blend	⅔ cup
1 cup	all-purpose flour	½ cup
1 cup	yellow cornmeal	½ cup
2 Tbsp.	sugar	1 Tbsp.
2½ tsp.	baking powder	1¼ tsp.
1 tsp.	salt	½ tsp.
2	egg(s), beaten	1
1⅓ cups	milk	⅔ cup
¼ cup	vegetable oil	2 Tbsp.
2 cups	red grape tomatoes, halved	1 cup
½ cup	coarsely snipped fresh cilantro	¼ cup
⅔ cup	pitted green olives, halved (optional)	⅓ cup

1 Preheat oven to 350°F. For 12 servings, grease two 2-quart baking dishes; set aside. In an extra-large skillet cook ground beef until browned, stirring to break up meat; drain off fat. Stir in undrained tomatoes and two-thirds of the corn; heat through. Divide mixture between prepared baking dishes. Sprinkle with 1 cup of the cheese.

2 For corn bread topping, in a large bowl combine flour, cornmeal, sugar, baking powder, and salt. In a bowl combine egg(s), milk, and oil. Stir into flour mixture until all is moistened. Evenly spread topping on meat mixture. Sprinkle the remaining cheese.

3 Bake, uncovered, about 30 minutes or until topping is set. Let stand for 5 minutes.

4 Meanwhile, in a bowl combine the remaining corn, the tomatoes, cilantro, and, if desired, olives. Serve with casserole.

For 6 servings: Prepare using method above, except assemble and bake in one 2-quart casserole. In Step 1 sprinkle casserole with ½ cup of the cheese.

PER SERVING: 506 cal., 27 g total fat (10 g sat. fat), 125 mg chol., 603 mg sodium, 38 g carbo., 2 g fiber, 30 g pro.

Easy Sheperd's Pie

Talk about a package deal. Every main ingredient—from beef and sauce to potatoes and cheese—comes from a package!

1 Preheat oven to 375°F. For 8 servings, grease a 3-quart rectangular baking dish. In a large saucepan, combine beef tips with gravy, frozen vegetables, soup, Worcestershire sauce, onion, thyme, and pepper. Bring to boiling over medium heat, stirring occasionally. Transfer mixture to the prepared baking dish.

3 Stir mashed potatoes to soften. Spoon potatoes in eight mounds on meat mixture. Sprinkle with cheese.

4 Bake, uncovered, for 20 to 25 minutes or until heated through. Let stand for 10 minutes before serving.

For 4 servings: Prepare using method above, except bake in a 2-quart casserole.

PER SERVING: 438 cal., 15 g total fat (6 g sat. fat), 64 mg chol., 1,570 mg sodium, 49 g carbo., 5 g fiber, 27 g pro.

PREP: 20 minutes   BAKE: 20 minutes
STAND: 10 minutes   OVEN: 375°F

8 servings	ingredients	4 servings
2 17-oz. pkg.	refrigerated cooked beef tips with gravy	1 17-oz. pkg.
4 cups	frozen vegetable blend (any combination)	2 cups
2 10.75-oz. cans	condensed tomato bisque soup	1 10.75-oz. can
2 Tbsp.	Worcestershire sauce	1 Tbsp.
2 tsp.	dried minced onion	1 tsp.
1 tsp.	dried thyme, crushed	1/2 tsp.
1/4 tsp.	black pepper	1/8 tsp.
2 20-oz. pkg.	refrigerated mashed potatoes	1 20-oz. pkg.
1 cup (4 oz.)	shredded cheddar cheese	1/2 cup (2 oz.)

Mexican-Style Moussaka

To hard-cook eggs perfectly, place eggs in a saucepan and cover with cold water. Bring to boiling; boil 1 minute. Cover pan, remove from heat and allow to stand 15 minutes. Cool eggs quickly in ice water; peel.

PREP: 25 minutes
BAKE: 30 minutes
STAND: 10 minutes
OVEN: 350°F

8 servings	ingredients	4 servings
2 lb.	lean ground beef	1 lb.
2 cups	chopped onion	1 cup
2 Tbsp.	all-purpose flour	1 Tbsp.
4 tsp.	chili powder	2 tsp.
1 tsp.	ground cumin	1/2 tsp.
1 tsp.	salt	1/2 tsp.
1/2 tsp.	ground black pepper	1/4 tsp.
4	hard-cooked eggs, coarsely chopped	2
2	egg(s), slightly beaten	1
1 14.75-oz. can	cream-style corn	1 8.25-oz. can

1 Preheat oven to 350°F. For 8 servings, in an extra-large skillet cook ground beef and onions until meat is browned and onions are tender, stirring to break up meat; drain off fat. Stir flour, chili powder, cumin, half the salt, and the pepper into meat mixture. Cook and stir for 1 minute. Stir in hard-cooked eggs. Transfer mixture to a 3-quart rectangular baking dish.

2 In a bowl combine slightly beaten egg(s), corn, and the remaining salt; spoon over meat mixture.

3 Bake, uncovered, about 30 minutes or just until center is set. Let stand for 10 minutes before serving.

For 4 servings: Prepare using method above, except use a large skillet and assemble and bake in a 1¹/₂-quart casserole.

PER SERVING: 367 cal., 21 g total fat (8 g sat. fat), 236 mg chol., 600 mg sodium, 17 g carbo., 2 g fiber, 28 g pro.

Upside-Down Pizza Casserole

Refrigerated biscuits bake to golden perfection on top of this cheesy-rich five-ingredient filling.

PREP: 25 minutes
BAKE: 15 minutes
OVEN: 400°F

10 servings	ingredients	5 servings
3 lb.	lean ground beef	1 1/2 lb.
2 15-oz. cans	Italian-style tomato sauce	1 15-oz. can
2 4-oz. cans	(drained weight) sliced mushrooms, drained	1 4-oz. can
1/2 cup	sliced pitted ripe olives (optional)	1/4 cup
2 to 3 cups (8 to 12 oz.)	shredded mozzarella cheese	1 to 1 1/2 cups (4 to 6 oz.)
2 10-oz. pkg. (10 biscuits each)	refrigerated biscuits	1 10-oz. pkg. (10 biscuits)

1 Preheat oven to 400°F. In an extra-large skillet cook ground beef until brown, stirring to break up meat. Drain off fat. Stir in tomato sauce, mushrooms, and, if desired, olives. Heat through. Divide mixture between two 2-quart rectangular baking dishes. Sprinkle with cheese.

2 Flatten each biscuit with your hands. Arrange the biscuits on top of cheese. Bake for 15 to 17 minutes or until biscuits are golden.

For 5 servings: Prepare using method above, except use a large skillet and assemble and bake in one 2-quart rectangular baking dish.

PER SERVING: 507 cal., 26 g total fat (10 g sat. fat), 103 mg chol., 1,251 mg sodium, 33 g carbo., 3 g fiber, 35 g pro.

Norwegian Meatballs

These magnificent meatballs—bathed in a sauce infused with the sweet, warm spiciness of nutmeg—are divine.

PREP: 35 minutes
BAKE: 30 minutes
OVEN: 350°F

10 servings	ingredients	5 servings
4	eggs, beaten	2
2½ cups	milk	1¼ cups
1⅓ cups (about 36 crackers)	crushed saltine crackers	⅔ cup (about 18 crackers)
⅔ cup	finely chopped onion	⅓ cup
1 tsp.	celery salt	½ tsp.
1 tsp.	ground nutmeg	½ tsp.
1 tsp.	ground black pepper	½ tsp.
4 lb.	lean ground beef	2 lb.
2 10.75-oz. cans	condensed cream of mushroom soup	1 10.75-oz. can

1 Preheat oven to 350°F. For 10 servings, grease two 3-quart rectangular baking dishes; set aside. In a bowl combine eggs and 1 cup of the milk. Stir in crushed crackers, onion, celery salt, half the nutmeg, and the pepper. Add ground beef; mix well. Shape mixture into 40 meatballs. Arrange meatballs in prepared baking dishes. Bake, uncovered, about 30 minutes or until done (an instant-read thermometer inserted in the meatballs registers 160°F).

2 For sauce, in a saucepan combine soup, the remaining milk, and the remaining nutmeg. Cook and stir over medium heat until heated through. Serve sauce over meatballs.

For 5 servings: Prepare using method above, except in Step 2 use ½ cup milk in the meatball mixture and shape mixture into 20 meatballs. Bake in one 3-quart rectangular baking dish.

PER SERVING: 469 cal., 26 g total fat (10 g sat. fat), 204 mg chol., 842 mg sodium, 17 g carbo., 1 g fiber, 39 g pro.

Ravioli-Dried Tomato Casserole

Reserve the flavorful oil from oil-packed dried tomatoes—it makes a scrumptious stand-in for plain olive oil when making homemade salad dressings and vinaigrettes.

PREP: 25 minutes
CHILL: 8 to 24 hours
BAKE: 40 minutes
STAND: 10 minutes
OVEN: 350°F

12 servings	ingredients	8 servings
2 9-oz. pkgs.	refrigerated four cheese or beef ravioli	1 9-oz. pkg.
½ 8-oz. jar	oil-packed dried tomatoes, drained and chopped	⅓ 8-oz. jar
1½ cups (6 oz.)	shredded cheddar cheese	1 cup (4 oz.)
1½ cups (6 oz.)	shredded Monterey Jack cheese	1 cup (4 oz.)
½ cup	grated Parmesan cheese	⅓ cup
8	eggs, beaten	6
2½ cups	milk	1⅔ cups
1 to 2 Tbsp.	snipped fresh basil or flat-leaf (Italian) parsley	2 to 4 tsp.

1 For 12 servings, grease a 3-quart rectangular baking dish. Evenly arrange uncooked ravioli in dish. Sprinkle with tomatoes. Top with cheddar cheese, Monterey Jack cheese, and Parmesan cheese; set aside. In a bowl whisk together eggs and milk. Pour over layers in dish. Cover; refrigerate for 8 to 24 hours.

2 Preheat oven to 350°F. Bake, uncovered, about 40 minutes or until top is golden and center is set. Let stand for 10 minutes. Sprinkle with basil.

For 8 servings: Prepare using method above, except assemble and bake in a 2-quart rectangular baking dish.

PER SERVING: 353 cal., 21 g total fat (11 g sat. fat), 213 mg chol., 490 mg sodium, 20 g carbo., 1 g fiber, 21 g pro.

Hearty Chili

To add a riot of color and lots of vitamin C to this slow cooker stunner, chop up a trio of red, yellow, and green sweet peppers.

PREP: 15 minutes
COOK: 10 to 12 hours (low)
or 5 to 6 hours (high)

10 servings	ingredients	5 servings
2 lb.	boneless beef round steak or boneless pork shoulder	1 lb.
2 cups	chopped onion	1 cup
1½ cups	chopped yellow, red, and/or green sweet peppers	¾ cup
2 15-oz. cans	chili beans with chili gravy	1 15-oz. can
2 14.5-oz. cans	stewed tomatoes, undrained and cut up	1 14.5-oz. can
1 15.5-oz. can	red kidney beans or pinto beans, rinsed and drained	1 cup
1 cup	beer or beef broth	½ cup
2 to 3 tsp.	chopped canned chipotle chile peppers in adobo sauce (see note, page 52)	1 to 1½ tsp.
2 tsp.	garlic salt	1 tsp.
2 tsp.	ground cumin	1 tsp.
1 tsp.	dried oregano, crushed	½ tsp.
	Shredded cheddar cheese, chopped onion, and/or sour cream (optional)	

1 Trim fat from meat and cut into ½-inch cubes. For 10 servings, in a 5½- or 6-quart slow cooker combine meat, onion, sweet peppers, chili beans in chili gravy, undrained tomatoes, kidney beans, beer, chile peppers, garlic salt, cumin, and oregano.

2 Cover and cook on low-heat setting for 10 to 12 hours or on high-heat setting for 5 to 6 hours. Spoon off fat. If desired, serve with cheese, onion, and/or sour cream.

For 5 servings: Prepare using method above, except use a 3½- to 4-quart slow cooker.

PER SERVING: 296 cal., 5 g total fat (1 g sat. fat), 52 mg chol., 821 mg sodium, 34 g carbo., 8 g fiber, 29 g pro.

Roast Beef Tamale Casserole

The flavor of poblano chile peppers varies from mild to snappy. Generally the darker the skin, the more intense the flavor.

PREP: 30 minutes **BAKE:** 25 minutes
STAND: 5 minutes **OVEN:** 350°F

8 servings	ingredients	4 servings
2 17-oz. pkg.	refrigerated cooked beef roast au jus	1 17-oz. pkg.
	Water	
¼ cup	butter	2 Tbsp.
1 cup	chopped onion	½ cup
2 medium	poblano or Anaheim peppers, seeded and sliced (see note, page 52)	1 medium
¼ cup	all-purpose flour	2 Tbsp.
2 15.5-oz. cans	pinto beans, rinsed and drained	1 15.5-oz. can
3 cups	zucchini and/or yellow summer squash cut in 1-inch pieces	1½ cups
2 cups	red grape tomatoes, halved	1 cup
1½ 16-oz. tubes	refrigerated cooked polenta, cut in ½-inch slices	¾ 16-oz. tube
2 cups (8 oz.)	shredded Monterey Jack cheese with jalapeño peppers	1 cup (4 oz.)
1 8-oz. carton	sour cream	½ cup
2 Tbsp.	snipped fresh cilantro	1 Tbsp.
	Lime wedges	

1 Preheat oven to 350°F. For 8 servings, lightly grease two 2-quart square baking dishes. Heat beef according to package directions. Pour juices into a 2-cup glass measure; add water to equal 2 cups. Set aside. Using two forks, coarsely shred beef.

2 In a large skillet melt butter over medium heat. Add onion and poblano pepper; cook in hot butter until tender. Stir in flour. Add juice mixture; cook until thickened and bubbly. Stir in beef, beans, zucchini, and tomatoes. Divide mixture between prepared baking dishes. Arrange polenta slices around edges of baking dishes.

3 Bake, uncovered, for 20 minutes. Sprinkle with cheese. Bake for 5 to 10 minutes more or until cheese is melted. Let stand for 5 minutes before serving.

4 Meanwhile, in a bowl combine sour cream and cilantro. Serve with casserole. Pass lime wedges.

For 4 servings: Prepare using method above, except assemble and bake in one 2-quart square baking dish.

PER SERVING: 578 cal., 31 g total fat (18 g sat. fat), 125 mg chol., 1,155 mg sodium, 40 g carbo., 8 g fiber, 41 g pro.

Frankfurter-Pasta Casserole

Kids who love hot dogs and macaroni will line up for this chunky, cheesy, casserole.

1 Preheat oven to 350°F. Cook macaroni according to package directions; drain. Set aside.

2 For 12 servings, in an extra-large skillet melt butter over medium heat. Add onions and garlic; cook in hot butter until nearly tender. Stir in frankfurters and cook until light brown. Stir in spaghetti sauce, tomatoes, and mushrooms. Bring to boiling. Remove from heat. Stir in sour cream, half the provolone cheese, and half the mozzarella cheese. Stir mixture into the drained pasta. Divide between two 2-quart casseroles. Cover casseroles.

3 Bake about 30 minutes or until hot. Uncover; sprinkle with the remaining provolone and mozzarella cheeses. Bake, uncovered, about 5 minutes more or until cheese is melted.

For 6 servings: Prepare using method above, except use a large skillet and bake in one 2-quart casserole.

PER SERVING: 600 cal., 38 g total fat (18 g sat. fat), 73 mg chol., 1,411 mg sodium, 46 g carbo., 4 g fiber, 21 g pro.

PREP: 30 minutes
BAKE: 35 minutes
OVEN: 350°F

12 servings	ingredients	6 servings
5⅓ cups (16 oz.)	dried medium shell macaroni	2⅔ cups (8 oz.)
2 Tbsp.	butter or margarine	1 Tbsp.
2 cups	chopped onion	1 cup
2 cloves	garlic, minced	1 clove
2 16-oz. pkg.	beef frankfurters, halved lengthwise and sliced	1 16-oz. pkg.
3 cups	purchased spaghetti sauce	1½ cups
2 cups	chopped fresh tomatoes	1 cup
2 4-oz. cans	(drained weight) mushroom stems and pieces, drained	1 4-oz. can
1 16-oz. carton	sour cream	1 8-oz. carton
1 cup (4 oz.)	shredded provolone cheese	½ cup (2 oz.)
1 cup (4 oz.)	shredded mozzarella cheese	½ cup (2 oz.)

Reuben Sandwich Casserole

Using deli-sliced corned beef makes this gloriously gooey casserole go together in a matter of minutes.

1 Preheat oven to 375°F. In a bowl combine sauerkraut, onion, parsley flakes, and caraway seeds. Evenly spread sauerkraut mixture in a 3-quart rectangular baking dish or eight 10- to 12-ounce individual gratin dishes.

2 Top with half the cheese, half the salad dressing, and the corned beef. Top with the remaining salad dressing and cheese.

3 In a bowl toss bread cubes with melted butter to coat. Sprinkle bread cubes over casseroles.

4 Bake, uncovered, about 35 minutes or until heated through and bread cubes are browned.

For 4 servings: Prepare using method above, except assemble and bake in a 1½-quart gratin dish or four 10- to 12-ounce individual gratin dishes.

PER SERVING: 596 cal., 45 g total fat (18 g sat. fat), 120 mg chol., 3,872 mg sodium, 22 g carbo., 10 g fiber, 26 g pro.

PREP: 20 minutes
BAKE: 35 minutes
OVEN: 375°F

8 servings	ingredients	4 servings
1 32-oz. jar	sauerkraut, rinsed and drained	1 16-oz. jar
½ cup	chopped onion	¼ cup
4 tsp.	dried parsley flakes, crushed	2 tsp.
2 tsp.	caraway seeds	1 tsp.
4 cups (16 oz.)	shredded Swiss cheese	2 cups (8 oz.)
1⅓ cups	bottled Thousand Island salad dressing	⅔ cup
12 oz.	thinly sliced cooked corned beef, coarsely chopped	6 oz.
6 slices	rye bread, cut into ½-inch cubes	3 slices
¼ cup	butter or margarine, melted	2 Tbsp.

Citrus-Corned Beef Sandwiches

Corned beef is cured in seasoned brine. Its subtly salty, bay leaf-infused flavor is exceedingly delicious when paired with a zesty orange sauce.

PREP: 35 minutes   COOK: 8 to 10 hours (low) or 4 to 5 hours (high)

16 sandwiches	ingredients	8 sandwiches
1 4- to 5-lb.	corned beef brisket with spice packet	1 2- to 3-lb.
2 cups	water	1 cup
½ cup	Dijon-style mustard	¼ cup
1 tsp.	finely shredded orange peel	½ tsp.
1⅓ cups	orange juice	⅔ cup
¼ cup	all-purpose flour	2 Tbsp.
32/16	slices marble rye bread or kaiser rolls, split	16/8
16 thin slices (about 12 oz.)	Muenster cheese	8 thin slices (about 6 oz.)
	Lettuce leaves (optional)	
	Orange slices (optional)	

1 Trim fat from meat. Sprinkle contents of spice packet over brisket; rub in with your fingers. For 16 sandwiches, place brisket in a 5- to 6-quart slow cooker. In a bowl combine the water and Dijon mustard; pour over brisket. Cover and cook on low-heat setting for 8 to 10 hours or on high-heat setting for 4 to 5 hours. Remove meat; cover to keep warm. Strain juices, reserving liquid; discard any solids.

2 For orange sauce, in a saucepan whisk together orange peel, orange juice, and flour. Gradually stir 1 cup of the reserved cooking juices into the mixture in the saucepan. Cook and stir until thickened and bubbly. Cook and stir for 1 minute more. Remove from heat.

3 To serve, preheat broiler. Scrape any whole spices from surface of brisket. Thinly slice meat across the grain. Place bread slices, cut sides up, on a very large baking sheet. Broil 4 inches from heat for 1 to 2 minutes or until toasted. Place sliced meat on 16 of the bread slices. Drizzle about 2 Tbsp. of the orange sauce over the meat on bread slices. Top with cheese. Broil for 1 to 2 minutes more or until cheese is melted. If desired, top with lettuce leaves and orange slices Add remaining bread slices.

For 8 sandwiches: Prepare using method above, except use a 3½- or 4-quart slow cooker. In Step 2 add ½ cup reserved cooking juices to mixture in saucepan.

PER SANDWICH: 463 cal., 22 g total fat (8 g sat. fat), 78 mg chol., 1,383 mg sodium, 35 g carbo., 1 g fiber, 29 g pro.

Zucchini-Pork Chop Supper

Gardeners who are familiar with the abundance of late-summer zucchini will relish this recipe. It is a tasty way to serve this versatile veggie.

1 Preheat oven to 350°F. For 12 servings, grease two 3-quart rectangular baking dishes; set aside. In a large bowl combine 15 cups of the croutons and the melted butter; toss gently to coat. Spread one-fourth of the buttered croutons in each baking dish. Set aside.

2 In another large bowl combine zucchini, soup, sour cream, two-thirds of the milk, the carrot, parsley, and pepper. Evenly spoon over buttered croutons in baking dishes. Sprinkle with the remaining buttered croutons.

3 Pour the remaining milk into a shallow dish. Coarsely crush the remaining croutons; place in another shallow dish. Trim fat from chops. Dip chops into milk, then into crushed croutons, turning to coat on both sides. Place chops on layers in baking dishes. Sprinkle with any remaining crushed croutons.

4 Bake, uncovered, for 50 to 60 minutes or until chops are slightly pink in center and juices run clear (160°F).

For 6 servings: Prepare using method above, except in Step 1 combine 7¹/₂ cups of the croutons with the melted butter and spread half the buttered croutons in one 3-quart rectangular baking dish.

PER SERVING: 639 cal., 24 g total fat (10 g sat. fat), 130 mg chol., 1,417 mg sodium, 57 g carbo., 4 g fiber, 46 g pro.

PREP: 35 minutes
BAKE: 50 minutes
OVEN: 350°F

12 servings	ingredients	6 servings
2 14-oz. pkg.	herb-seasoned stuffing croutons	1 14-oz. pkg.
¹/₂ cup	butter or margarine, melted	¹/₄ cup
8 cups	coarsely chopped zucchini	4 cups
2 10.75-oz. cans	condensed cream of celery soup	1 10.75-oz. can
1 16-oz. carton	light sour cream	1 8-oz. carton
1¹/₂ cups	milk	³/₄ cup
1 cup	shredded carrot	¹/₂ cup
2 Tbsp.	snipped fresh parsley	1 Tbsp.
¹/₂ to 1 tsp.	ground black pepper	¹/₄ to ¹/₂ tsp.
12	bone-in pork loin chops, cut ³/₄ inch thick	6

Pork Soft Shell Tacos

No need for charcoal or matches—chipotle chile powder is all you'll need to imbue this skillet-cooked pork with smoky flavor.

START TO FINISH: 25 minutes

8 servings	ingredients	4 servings
1 lb.	boneless pork loin	8 oz.
1 Tbsp.	vegetable oil	2 tsp.
½ cup	light sour cream	¼ cup
½ tsp.	chipotle chile powder	¼ tsp.
8	flour tortillas, warmed if desired	4
1 cup	shredded lettuce	½ cup
1 cup	diced tomato	½ cup
1 cup (4 oz.)	shredded reduced-fat cheddar cheese	½ cup (2 oz.)
	Salsa	

1 If desired, partially freeze pork for easier slicing. Trim fat from meat. Thinly slice meat across the grain into bite-size strips. For 8 servings, in a very large skillet cook pork in hot oil over medium-high heat until brown; set aside.

2 In a small bowl combine sour cream and chipotle chili powder; set aside.

3 Spoon one-fourth of the meat onto each tortilla just below the center. Top meat with lettuce, tomato, and cheese. Fold top half of each tortilla over filling. Serve with sour cream mixture and salsa.

For 4 servings: Prepare using method above, except use a large skillet.

PER SERVING: 240 cal., 11 g total fat (4g sat. fat), 48 mg chol., 263 mg sodium, 14 g carbo., 1 g fiber, 19 g pro.

Santa Fe Pork Pie

In New Mexico, the residents love their green chiles and use them often. This simple, scrumptious pie showcases the subtle heat of green chiles.

1 Preheat oven to 425°F. In a saucepan combine broth, potatoes, celery, and garlic. Bring to boiling; reduce heat. Simmer, covered, for 8 to 10 minutes or until potatoes are nearly tender. Do not drain.

2 Meanwhile, for filling, in a bowl combine chili powder and thyme. Add pork cubes; toss to coat. For 12 servings, in an extra-large skillet heat oil over medium heat. Add half the pork; cook in hot oil for 4 to 5 minutes or until no longer pink. Using a slotted spoon; remove meat from skillet; set aside. Repeat with remaining meat; drain. Return all meat to skillet. Add potato mixture, chile peppers, and cilantro. Bring to boiling. Divide mixture between two 2-quart casseroles.

3 Snip each biscuit in 4 pieces; arrange on top of hot mixture. Bake, uncovered, about 15 minutes or until biscuits are golden. If desired, top with sour cream.

For 6 servings: Prepare using method above, except assemble and bake in one 2-quart casserole.

PER SERVING: 240 cal., 10 g total fat (2 g sat. fat), 45 mg chol., 388 mg sodium, 18 g carbo., 2 g fiber, 19 g pro.

PREP: 35 minutes
BAKE: 15 minutes
OVEN: 425°F

12 servings	ingredients	6 servings
2²⁄₃ cups	chicken broth	1¹⁄₃ cups
6 medium	potatoes, peeled and cut in ½-inch cubes	3 medium
1 cup	sliced celery	½ cup
8 cloves	garlic, minced	4 cloves
4 tsp.	chili powder	2 tsp.
2 tsp.	dried thyme, crushed	1 tsp.
2 lb.	boneless pork loin, cut in ¾-inch cubes	1 lb.
¼ cup	vegetable oil	2 Tbsp.
2 4-oz. cans	diced green chile peppers, drained	1 4-oz. can
8 tsp.	dried cilantro, crushed	4 tsp.
2 7.5-oz. pkg. (10 each)	refrigerated biscuits	1 7.5-oz. pkg. (10)
Sour cream (optional)		

Potato-Ham Bake

To trim asparagus spears, grasp a spear with one hand on the tapered end and one on the stem end. Bend until the stem breaks easily. The spear will naturally break to separate the tender spear from the tough stem.

PREP: 30 minutes
BAKE: 30 minutes
STAND: 5 minutes
OVEN: 400°F

8 servings	ingredients	4 servings
2 lb.	Yukon gold potatoes, sliced	1 lb.
2 8-oz. tubs	light cream cheese spread with chive and onion	1 8-oz. tub
1½ cups	milk	¾ cup
½ cup (2 oz.)	finely shredded Parmesan cheese	¼ cup (1 oz.)
½ tsp.	ground black pepper	¼ tsp
2 Tbsp.	snipped fresh tarragon	1 Tbsp.
1 lb.	cooked boneless ham, cut in bite-size pieces	8 oz.
2 lb.	fresh asparagus spears, trimmed and cut in 2- to 3-inch pieces	1 lb.
	Tarragon sprigs (optional)	

1 Preheat oven to 400°F. In a covered saucepan cook potatoes in small amount of lightly salted boiling water for 5 to 7 minute or just until tender. Drain. Remove potatoes from saucepan; set aside.

2 For sauce, in the same saucepan combine cream cheese, milk, half the Parmesan cheese, and the pepper. Whisk over low heat until mixture is smooth and cheese is melted. Remove from heat; stir in snipped tarragon.

3 For 8 servings, layer potatoes, ham, asparagus, and sauce in 3-quart rectangular baking dish. Cover with foil.

4 Bake for 20 minutes. Uncover; sprinkle with the remaining Parmesan cheese. Bake for 10 to 12 minutes more or until heated through. Let stand for 5 minutes before serving. If desired, top with tarragon sprigs.

For 4 servings: Prepare using method above, except assemble and bake in one 1½-quart gratin dish.

PER SERVING: 346 cal., 16 g total fat (9 g sat. fat), 67 mg chol., 1,162 mg sodium, 30 g carbo., 5 g fiber, 22 g pro.

Ham Balls in Barbecue Sauce

Decisions, decisions. Should you serve these glistening gems with buttered spaetzle over fluffy cooked rice—or eat them from toothpicks before they even make it to the table?

PREP: 25 minutes
BAKE: 45 minutes
OVEN: 350°F

12 servings	ingredients	6 servings
4	eggs, beaten	2
3 cups	soft bread crumbs	1½ cups
1 cup	finely chopped onion	½ cup
¼ cup	milk	2 Tbsp.
4 tsp.	dry mustard	2 tsp.
½ tsp.	ground black pepper	¼ tsp.
1½ lb.	ground cooked ham	12 oz.
1½ lb.	ground pork or ground beef	12 oz.
1½ cups	packed brown sugar	¾ cup
1 cup	ketchup	½ cup
¼ cup	vinegar	2 Tbsp.

1 Preheat oven to 350°F. For 12 servings, lightly grease two 2-quart rectangular baking dishes; set aside. In a large bowl combine eggs, bread crumbs, onion, milk, half the mustard, and the pepper. Add ground ham and ground pork; mix well. Shape into balls, using about ⅓ cup mixture for each. Place ham balls in prepared baking dishes.

2 In a bowl combine brown sugar, ketchup, vinegar, and the remaining mustard. Stir until sugar is dissolved. Pour over hamballs.

3 Bake, uncovered, about 45 minutes or until done (an instant-read thermometer inserted in the hamballs registers 160°F).

For 6 servings: Prepare using method above, except bake hamballs in one 2-quart rectangular baking dish.

PER SERVING: 427 cal., 19 g total fat (7 g sat. fat), 143 mg chol., 1,107 mg sodium, 42 g carbo., 1 g fiber, 23 g pro.

Denver Potato Casserole

The buttery flavor and tender texture of Yukon gold potatoes make this tater casserole a treat for brunch or supper.

1 Preheat oven to 350°F. For 8 servings, grease two 2-quart square baking dishes. Layer one-fourth the potatoes, one-fourth the ham, one-fourth the sweet pepper, one-fourth the onion, and one-fourth the cheese in each baking dish. Repeat layers with the remaining ham, sweet pepper, and onion. Top with the remaining potatoes. Cover baking dishes with foil.

2 Bake for 45 minutes. Uncover and bake about 15 minutes more or until potatoes are tender. Sprinkle with remaining cheese. Bake, uncovered, about 5 minutes more or until cheese is melted.

For 4 servings: Prepare using method above, except in Step 1, use one 2-quart baking dish and layer half the potatoes, half the ham, half the sweet pepper, half the onion, and half the cheese in baking dish. Repeat with remaining ham, sweet pepper, and onion. Top with remaining potatoes.

PER SERVING: 315 cal., 12 g total fat (6 g sat. fat), 56 mg chol., 1,010 mg sodium, 27 g carbo., 3 g fiber, 24 g pro.

PREP: 20 minutes
BAKE: 65 minutes
OVEN: 350°F

8 servings	ingredients	4 servings
8 medium (2²/₃ lb. total)	Yukon gold potatoes, thinly sliced	4 medium (1¹/₃ lb. total)
1 lb.	cubed cooked ham	8 oz.
1¹/₂ cups	chopped green sweet pepper	³/₄ cup
²/₃ cup	chopped sweet onion	¹/₃ cup
2 cups (8 oz.)	shredded Colby-Monterey Jack cheese	1 cup (4 oz.)

Ham and Cheese Lasagna

Layers of smoky ham and earthy mushrooms blend with red wine to give this lasagna unique, complex flavor.

1 Preheat oven to 350°F. For sauce, in an extra-large skillet heat oil over medium heat. Add celery, carrots, onion, and garlic; cook and stir in hot oil for 10 minutes or just until vegetables are tender. Add mushrooms and ham. Cook, uncovered, for 10 minutes, stirring occasionally. Stir in cream, undrained tomatoes, the water, and wine. Bring to boiling; reduce heat. Simmer, uncovered, for 5 minutes. Season to taste with salt and pepper.

2 In a bowl combine Swiss cheese and Parmesan cheese. For 12 servings, spoon one-fourth of the sauce in a 3-quart rectangular baking dish. Sprinkle with one-fourth of the cheese mixture. Top with with one-third of the lasagna noodles, overlapping to fit. Repeat layers twice. Spoon on remaining sauce and sprinkle with remaining cheese mixture. Cover tightly with foil.

3 Bake about 50 minutes or until heated through and noodles are tender when pierced with a fork. Let stand, covered, for 20 minutes before serving.

For 8 servings: Prepare using method above, except assemble and bake in a 2-quart rectangular baking dish.

PER SERVING: 376 cal., 25 g total fat (14 g sat. fat), 86 mg chol., 671 mg sodium, 22 g carbo., 2 g fiber, 15 g pro.

PREP: 1 hour
BAKE: 50 minutes
STAND: 20 minutes
OVEN: 350°F

12 servings	ingredients	8 servings
2 Tbsp.	olive oil	4 tsp.
2 cups	thinly sliced celery	1¹/₃ cups
2 cups	chopped carrots	1¹/₃ cups
1 cup	chopped onion	²/₃ cup
2 cloves	garlic, minced	1 clove
3 cups	sliced cremini mushrooms or other small brown mushrooms	2 cups
2 cups	cubed cooked ham	1¹/₃ cups
2 cups	whipping cream	1¹/₃ cups
1 14.5-oz. can	diced tomatoes with basil and garlic, undrained	1 cup
¹/₂ cup	water	¹/₃ cup
¹/₄ cup	dry red wine	3 Tbsp.
	Salt	
	Ground black pepper	
1¹/₂ cups (6 oz.)	shredded Swiss cheese	1 cup (4 oz.)
1 cup	grated Parmesan cheese	²/₃ cup
12	no-boil lasagna noodles	9

White Bean and Sausage Rigatoni

Budget-friendly kielbasa—also known as Polish Sausage—adds wonderful smokiness to this bake.

PREP: 25 minutes
BAKE: 30 minutes
OVEN: 375°F

12 servings	ingredients	6 servings
10 cups (16 oz.)	dried rigatoni	5 cups (8 oz.)
1 lb.	cooked kielbasa	8 oz.
1 6-oz. can	Italian-style tomato paste	½ a 6-oz. can
½ cup	dry red wine or reduced-sodium chicken broth	¼ cup
2 10-oz. pkg.	frozen chopped spinach, thawed and drained well	1 10-oz. pkg
4 14.5-oz. cans	diced tomatoes with basil and garlic, undrained	2 14.5-oz. cans
2 15.5-oz. cans	Great Northern beans, rinsed and drained	1 15.5-oz. can
⅔ cup (3 oz.)	shredded or grated Parmesan cheese	⅓ cup (1½ oz.)

1 Preheat oven to 375°F. Cook pasta according to package directions; drain. Return to saucepan. Cut kielbasa in half lengthwise and then in bias slices. In a bowl combine tomato paste and wine.

2 Add kielbasa, tomato paste mixture, spinach, undrained tomatoes, and beans to the cooked pasta; mix well. For 12 servings, divide mixture between two 3-quart rectangular baking dishes. Cover with foil.

3 Bake about 25 minutes or until heated through. Sprinkle with cheese. Bake, uncovered, about 5 minutes more or until cheese is melted.

For 6 servings: Prepare using method above, except bake in one 3-quart rectangular baking dish.

PER SERVING: 564 cal., 20 g total fat (11 g sat. fat), 48 mg chol., 1,706 mg sodium, 62 g carbo., 7 g fiber, 30 g pro.

Lasagna Blanca

These serving-size roll-ups not only look and taste great, but they're supersimple to prepare.

1 Preheat oven to 350°F. For 12 servings, grease a 3-quart rectangular baking dish; set aside. Cook lasagna noodles according to package directions; drain and rinse with cold water. Set aside.

2 Meanwhile, in a large skillet cook sausage, green onions, and mushrooms over medium heat until meat is cooked through, stirring to break up meat. Drain well; set aside.

3 For filling, in a bowl combine cottage cheese, cream cheese, one-third of the Monterey Jack cheese, the garlic powder, and half the pepper; set aside.

4 Spread filling evenly on one side of each noodle. Sprinkle sausage mixture on top. Roll up each noodle in a spiral. Place lasagna rolls, short end of noodle sides down, in the prepared baking dish; set aside.

5 For sauce, in a saucepan melt butter. Stir in flour, tarragon, and the remaining pepper. Add milk. Cook and stir until slightly thickened and bubbly. Remove from heat. Stir in half the remaining Monterey Jack cheese. Pour sauce over pasta rolls. Cover with foil.

6 Bake for 25 minutes. Uncover; sprinkle with the remaining Monterey Jack cheese. Bake about 10 minutes more or until heated through. Let stand for 10 minutes before serving.

For 8 servings: Prepare using method above, except assemble and bake in a 2-quart rectangular baking dish.

PER SERVING: 317 cal., 17 g total fat (9 g sat. fat), 54 mg chol., 378 mg sodium, 21 g carbo., 1 g fiber, 17 g pro.

PREP: 1 hour
BAKE: 35 minutes
STAND: 10 minutes
OVEN: 350°F

12 servings	ingredients	8 servings
12	dried lasagna noodles	8
1 lb.	spicy bulk pork sausage	12 oz.
1/2 cup	chopped green onions	1/3 cup
1/2 cup	chopped fresh mushrooms	1/3 cup
1 cup	cream-style cottage cheese	2/3 cup
1/2 an 8-oz. pkg.	cream cheese, softened	1 3-oz. pkg.
1 1/2 cups (6 oz.)	shredded Monterey Jack cheese or cheddar cheese	1 cup (4 oz.)
1/2 tsp.	garlic powder	1/4 tsp.
1/4 tsp.	ground black pepper	1/4 tsp.
1 Tbsp.	butter or margarine	1 Tbsp.
1 Tbsp.	all-purpose flour	1 Tbsp.
1/8 tsp.	dried tarragon, crushed	1/8 tsp.
1 cup	milk	1 cup

Picadillo Sandwiches

The slight sweetness of raisins contrasted with the savory saltiness of olives creates balance in this delicious sandwich version of traditional Spanish picadillo (peek-ah-DEE-yoh).

START TO FINISH: 35 minutes

12 servings	ingredients	6 servings
2 lb.	bulk pork sausage	1 lb.
2 cups	chopped onions	1 cup
2 14.5-oz. cans	diced tomatoes, undrained	1 14.5-oz. can
1 cup	golden raisins	1/2 cup
1/2 cup	chopped green olives	1/4 cup
1/4 cup	tomato paste	2 Tbsp.
2 Tbsp.	balsamic vinegar	1 Tbsp.
1 tsp.	ground cumin	1/2 tsp
1 tsp.	dried oregano, crushed	1/2 tsp.
1/4 tsp.	crushed red pepper (optional)	1/8 tsp.
12	hoagie buns, split and toasted	6
2 cups (8 oz.)	shredded Monterey Jack cheese	1 cup (4 oz.)

1 In an extra-large skillet cook sausage and onions for 10 minutes or until meat is browned and onions are tender, stirring to break up meat; drain off fat. Stir in undrained tomatoes, raisins, olives, tomato paste, vinegar, cumin, oregano, and, if using, crushed red pepper. Bring to boiling; reduce heat. Simmer, uncovered, for 10 minutes or until sauce is thickened.

2 Spoon sausage mixture into buns. Top with cheese.

PER SERVING: 750 cal., 29 g total fat (11 g sat. fat), 66 mg chol., 1,399 mg sodium, 91 g carbo., 6 g fiber, 28 g pro.

Italian-Style Spaghetti Squash

Let kids help with scooping the amazing golden strands from the baked squash halves. It's a fascinating feat!

1 Halve each squash crosswise; remove seeds. For 12 servings, place 1 squash, cut sides down, in a 2-quart rectangular baking dish. Add ¼ cup of the water. Cover with vented plastic wrap. Microwave on high (100 percent power) for 13 to 15 minutes or until squash is tender when pierced with fork, rearranging once for even cooking. Set aside. Repeat with the remaining squash and water.

2 In an extra-large skillet cook sausage, mushrooms, sweet pepper, onion, and garlic over medium heat until sausage is cooked through, stirring to break up sausage. Drain fat.

3 Preheat oven to 350°F. Scrape pulp from each squash (6 cups total). Wipe out baking dishes; coat with cooking spray. Spread one-fourth of the squash in each dish. Add one-fourth of the sausage mixture and one-fourth of the olives to each dish. Sprinkle with Italian seasoning and black pepper. Top each dish with one-fourth of the pasta sauce and one-fourth of the cheese. Repeat layers.

4 Bake, uncovered, for 30 minutes. Sprinkle with remaining cheese. Bake about 5 minutes or until cheese is melted. Let stand for 10 minutes. Sprinkle with parsley.

For 6 servings: Prepare using method above, except in Step 1 microwave one squash. In Step 3 use one 2-quart rectangular baking dish and layer half the squash, sausage, and olives in baking dish. Sprinkle with Italian seasoning and pepper. Top with half the pasta sauce and cheese. Repeat layers.

PER SERVING: 351 cal., 24 g total fat (11 g sat. fat), 64 mg chol., 941 mg sodium, 13 g carbo., 4 g fiber, 18 g pro.

**PREP: 35 minutes COOK: 26 minutes BAKE: 35 minutes
STAND: 10 minutes OVEN: 350°F**

12 servings	ingredients	6 servings
2 medium (2¼ lb. each)	spaghetti squash	1 medium (2¼ lb.)
½ cup	water	¼ cup
1½ lb.	bulk Italian sausage	12 oz.
3 cups	sliced fresh mushrooms	1½ cups
1½ cups	chopped green or red sweet pepper	¾ cup
⅔ cup	finely chopped onion	⅓ cup
6 cloves	garlic, minced	3 cloves
	Nonstick cooking spray	
2 4.25-oz. cans	chopped pitted ripe olives (optional)	1 4.25-oz. can
1 tsp.	dried Italian seasoning, crushed	½ tsp.
¼ tsp.	ground black pepper	⅛ tsp.
3 cups	purchased red pasta sauce	1½ cups
3 cups (12 oz.)	shredded Monterey Jack cheese, mozzarella cheese, or Italian-blend cheese	1½ cups (6 oz.)
½ cup	snipped fresh Italian (flat-leaf) parsley	¼ cup

Italian Polenta Casserole

Polenta—northern Italy's quintessential comfort food—is simply finely ground cornmeal cooked in water or broth. It is a wonderful flavor sponge that transports the tastes of any food it accompanies.

1 Preheat oven to 400°F. For 8 servings, lightly grease a 3-quart rectangular baking dish; set aside.

2 In a large saucepan bring broth and butter to boiling. Meanwhile, stir together the milk and polenta mix. Add polenta mixture to boiling broth. Cook and stir until bubbly; cook and stir for 3 to 5 minutes more or until very thick. Remove from heat. Stir in cream cheese, three-fourths of the mozzarella, and half the Parmesan until well mixed. Spread two-thirds of the polenta mixture in the prepared baking dish; set aside.

3 In a large skillet cook sausage, mushrooms, onion, and garlic until meat is browned and onion is tender, stirring to break up meat; drain off fat. Add pasta sauce; heat through. Spoon sausage mixture on polenta in baking dish, spreading evenly. Drop spoonfuls of remaining polenta on top of sauce and sprinkle with the remaining mozzarella and Parmesan cheese.

4 Bake, uncovered, about 20 minutes or until heated through and top is lightly golden.

For 6 servings: Prepare using method above, except assemble and bake in a 2-quart rectangular baking dish.

PER SERVING: 583 cal., 34 g total fat (18 g sat. fat), 92 mg chol., 1,933 mg sodium, 37 g carbo., 4 g fiber, 31 g pro.

PREP: 45 minutes
BAKE: 20 minutes
OVEN: 400°F

8 servings	ingredients	6 servings
2½ cups	chicken broth	1⅔ cups
3 Tbsp.	butter or margarine	2 Tbsp.
2 cups	milk	1⅓ cups
1½ cups	quick-cooking polenta mix	1 cup
1 3-oz. pkg.	cream cheese, cut up	2 oz.
1 cup (4 oz.)	shredded mozzarella or provolone cheese	⅔ cup (2½ oz.)
½ cup (2 oz.)	finely shredded or grated Parmesan cheese	⅓ cup (1½ oz.)
12 oz.	bulk sweet or hot Italian sausage	8 oz.
1 cup	mushrooms, quartered	⅔ cup
1 medium	onion, cut in thin wedges	1 small
2 cloves	garlic, minced	1 clove
2 cups	purchased pasta sauce	1⅓ cups

HOMETOWN FAVORITES

Chapter

4

SELECT SEAFOOD ENTRÉES

RECIPE FINDER

p.120   p.124
p.129   p.130
p.132   p.135

FOR MORE RECIPES:
Visit BHG.com/Recipes

Chilly Bow Ties and Tuna, p.125

Trout Amandine

Coarse, crisp panko crumbs and buttery almonds provide the supercrunchy crust on these fish fillets.

PREP: 15 minutes
BAKE: 4 to 6 minutes per ¹/₂-inch thickness
OVEN: 450°F

8 servings	ingredients	4 servings
8 4-oz.	fresh or frozen skinless cod, tilapia, trout, or halibut fillets, ¹/₂ to 1 inch thick	4 4-oz.
¹/₂ cup	buttermilk or milk	¹/₄ cup
1 cup	panko (Japanese-style) bread crumbs or fine dry bread crumbs	¹/₂ cup
¹/₄ cup	snipped fresh parsley	2 Tbsp.
1 tsp.	dry mustard	¹/₂ tsp.
¹/₂ tsp.	salt	¹/₄ tsp.
¹/₄ tsp.	ground black pepper	¹/₈ tsp.
¹/₂ cup	sliced almonds, coarsely chopped	¹/₄ cup
2 Tbsp.	butter, melted	1 Tbsp.

1 Thaw fish, if frozen. Preheat oven to 450°F. Grease a shallow baking pan; set aside. Rinse fish; pat dry with paper towels. Measure thickness of fish.

2 In a shallow dish pour in buttermilk. In another shallow dish combine bread crumbs, parsley, dry mustard, salt, and pepper. Dip fish into buttermilk, then coat both sides of fish with crumb mixture. Place coated fish in prepared baking pan. Sprinkle fish with almonds. Drizzle melted butter over fish.

3 Bake, uncovered, for 4 to 6 minutes per ¹/₂-inch thickness of fish or until fish begins to flake easily when tested with a fork.

PER SERVING: 200 cal., 8 g total fat (2 g sat. fat), 56 mg chol., 266 mg sodium, 8 g carbo., 1 g fiber, 24 g pro.

Sesame-Crusted Cod

For a shining example of healthful eating, serve lean cod, snappy green beans, and fresh citrus.

1 Thaw fish, if frozen. Preheat broiler. Rinse fish; pat dry with paper towels. For 8 servings, cut in eight serving-size portions, if necessary. Place fish on the unheated rack of a broiler pan; sprinkle with salt and pepper.

2 In a bowl combine butter and sesame seeds; measure 2 tablespoons and set aside for bean mixture. Brush fish with half the remaining butter-sesame seed mixture.

3 Broil fish 5 to 6 inches from the heat about 8 minutes or until fish begins to flake easily when tested with a fork, turning and brushing fish with remaining half of butter-sesame seed mixture halfway through cooking.

4 Meanwhile, in a skillet heat the reserved 2 tablespoons butter-sesame seed mixture over medium-high heat. Add green beans and orange slices. Cook, covered, for 2 minutes. Uncover; add garlic. Cook and stir, uncovered, for 5 to 6 minutes more or until beans are crisp-tender. Serve bean mixture with fish.

For 4 servings: Prepare using method above, except cut in four serving-size portions, if necessary. In a small bowl combine butter and sesame seeds; measure 1 tablespoon of the mixture and set aside for bean mixture.

PER SERVING: 241 cal., 12 g total fat (6 g sat. fat), 72 mg chol., 274 mg sodium, 12 g carbo., 4 g fiber, 23 g pro.

PREP: 20 minutes
BROIL: 8 minutes

8 servings	ingredients	4 servings
2 lb.	fresh or frozen skinless cod, haddock, or other fish fillets, ³⁄₄ inch thick	1 lb.
	Salt	
	Ground black pepper	
¹⁄₃ cup	butter, melted	3 Tbsp.
¹⁄₄ cup	sesame seeds	2 Tbsp.
2 12-oz. pkg.	trimmed fresh tender young green beans	1 12-oz. pkg.
2 medium	orange(s), halved and sliced	1 medium
6 cloves	garlic, thinly sliced	3 cloves

Tuna Noodle Casserole

Give Mom's well-received standby an update with piquant Dijon-style mustard and robust roasted red peppers.

PREP: 25 minutes
BAKE: 20 minutes
STAND: 5 minutes
OVEN: 375°F

8 servings	ingredients	4 servings
6 cups	medium noodles	3 cups
2 cups	chopped celery	1 cup
½ cup	chopped onion	¼ cup
½ cup	butter	¼ cup
½ cup	all-purpose flour	¼ cup
¼ cup	Dijon-style mustard	2 Tbsp.
½ tsp.	ground black pepper	¼ tsp.
4½ cups	milk	2¼ cups
2 12- to 12.25-oz. cans	chunk white tuna (water pack), drained and broken in chunks	1 12- to 12.25-oz. can
1 cup	chopped bottled roasted red sweet peppers	½ cup
	Potato chips, optional	

1 Preheat oven to 375°F. Cook noodles according to package directions. Drain. Return noodles to hot pan; cover and keep warm.

2 For sauce, in saucepan cook celery and onion in hot butter over medium heat until tender. Stir in flour, mustard, and black pepper. Add milk all at once. Cook and stir until slightly thickened and bubbly, whisking to remove any lumps.

3 Gently fold sauce, tuna, and red sweet peppers into warm noodles. For 8 servings, transfer mixture to a lightly greased 3-quart rectangular baking dish. If desired, top with chips.

4 Bake, uncovered, for 20 to 30 minutes or until heated through and top is golden. Let stand for 5 minutes before serving.

For 4 servings: Prepare using method above, except transfer to a lightly greased 1½-quart baking dish.

PER SERVING: 419 cal., 16 g total fat (10 g sat. fat), 110 mg chol., 720 mg sodium, 36 g carbo., 2 g fiber, 29 g pro.

Tuna with Cheese Biscuits

Tuna—the reliable pantry pal—becomes a taste treat when topped with miunds of savory cheese biscuit batter.

PREP: 15 minutes
BAKE: 30 minutes
OVEN: 425°F

8 servings	ingredients	4 servings
1 cup	chopped onion	½ cup
1 cup	chopped green sweet pepper	½ cup
⅓ cup	butter	3 Tbsp.
2 10.75-oz. cans	condensed cream of chicken soup	1 10.75-oz. can
2 cups	milk	1 cup
2 9- to 9.25-oz. cans	tuna, drained and flaked	1 9- to 9.25 can
4 tsp.	lemon juice	2 tsp.
2 7.75-oz. packets	cheese-garlic or three-cheese complete biscuit mix	1 7.75-oz. packet
	Snipped green onions or chives	

1 Preheat oven to 425°F. In a saucepan cook onion and sweet pepper in hot butter over medium heat until tender. Gently stir in soup and milk. Cook and stir until bubbly. Stir in tuna and lemon juice.

2 For 8 servings, transfer mixture to an ungreased 3-quart rectangular baking dish. Bake, uncovered, for 15 minutes.

3 Meanwhile, prepare biscuit mix according to package directions. Drop batter in 20 to 22 mounds on hot tuna mixture. Bake, uncovered, for 15 to 20 minutes more or until biscuits are golden and a wooden toothpick inserted in centers of biscuits comes out clean. Garnish with green onions.

For 4 servings: Prepare using method above, except transfer mixture to an ungreased 1½-quart casserole. Bake, uncovered, for 15 minutes. Drop batter in 10 to 12 mounds on hot tuna mixture.

PER SERVING: 564 cal., 31 g total fat (12 g sat. fat), 46 mg chol., 1,470 mg sodium, 45 g carbo., 1 g fiber, 26 g pro.

Chilly Bow Ties and Tuna

Juicy mandarin oranges and crunchy pea pods take this tuna pasta salad from mundane to marvelous—and make it ideal to carry for lunch.

1 Cook pasta according to package directions. Drain. Rinse with cold water; drain again. Transfer to a bowl.

2 Meanwhile, for dressing, in a bowl combine mayonnaise, Italian dressing, green onions (if using), orange juice, salt, and pepper.

3 Add dressing to pasta; toss lightly to combine. Gently fold in orange sections, tuna, and pea pods. Cover and refrigerate for 4 to 24 hours. Before serving, if necessary, stir in a little milk to moisten.

PER SERVING: 254 cal., 3 g total fat (1 g sat. fat), 13 mg chol., 433 mg sodium, 43 g carbo., 2 g fiber, 13 g pro.

PREP: 15 minutes
CHILL: 4 to 24 hours

12 servings	ingredients	6 servings
1 lb.	dried farfalle pasta (bow ties)	8 oz.
²/₃ cup	light mayonnaise or salad dressing	¹/₃ cup
²/₃ cup	bottled reduced-calorie Italian salad dressing	¹/₃ cup
¹/₂ cup	thinly sliced green onions (optional)	¹/₄ cup
¹/₄ cup	orange juice	2 Tbsp.
¹/₂ tsp.	salt	¹/₄ tsp.
¹/₂ tsp.	ground black pepper	¹/₄ tsp.
2 11-oz. cans	mandarin orange sections, drained	1 11-oz. can
2 12- to 12.25-oz. cans	chunk white tuna (water pack), drained and broken in chunks	1 12- to 12.25-oz. can
2 cups	fresh pea pods, trimmed and halved lengthwise	1 cup
	Milk (optional)	

Smoky Salmon Casserole

Because of their high fat content, pine nuts do not keep well at room temperature. Store them in an airtight container in the refrigerator up to 3 months or freeze the nuts up to 9 months.

PREP: 30 minutes
BAKE: 30 minutes
STAND: 10 minutes
OVEN: 350°F

12 servings	ingredients	6 servings
16 oz.	dried bow tie pasta or penne pasta	8 oz.
2 cups	chopped red sweet peppers	1 cup
1 cup	chopped green onions	½ cup
¼ cup	butter	2 Tbsp.
¼ cup	all-purpose flour	2 Tbsp.
½ tsp.	black pepper	¼ tsp.
5 cups	milk	2½ cups
3 cups	shredded smoked Gouda cheese (6 oz.)	1½ cups
1 tsp.	finely shredded lemon peel	½ tsp.
2 Tbsp.	lemon juice	1 Tbsp.
2 14-oz. cans	quartered artichoke hearts, thawed	1 14-oz. can
2 4-oz. pieces	smoked salmon, flaked, skin and bones removed	1 4-oz. piece
2 cups	soft bread crumbs or panko (Japanese-style bread crumbs)	1 cup
½ cup	pine nuts	¼ cup
	Freshly ground black pepper	

1 Preheat oven to 350°F. Cook pasta according to package directions; drain. Set aside.

2 Meanwhile, in a large skillet cook sweet peppers and green onions in hot butter over medium heat about 3 minutes or until tender. For 12 servings, stir in flour and the ½ teaspoon pepper. Gradually stir in milk. Cook and stir until slightly thickened and bubbly. Gradually add cheese, stirring until melted. Stir in lemon peel and lemon juice (mixture may appear curdled).

3 In a large bowl combine cooked pasta, cheese mixture, artichoke hearts, and smoked salmon. Transfer mixture to an ungreased 3-quart baking dish.

4 Sprinkle casserole with bread crumbs, pine nuts, and freshly ground pepper. Bake, uncovered, for 30 to 35 minutes or until mixture is heated through and crumbs are golden. Let stand for 10 minutes before serving.

For 6 servings: Prepare using method above, except in Step 2 use ¼ teaspoon pepper. Transfer mixture to an ungreased 2-quart baking dish and bake, uncovered, for 25 to 30 minutes or until mixture is heated through and crumbs are golden. Let stand for 10 minutes before serving.

PER SERVING: 470 cal., 19 g total fat (10 g sat. fat), 74 mg chol., 780 mg sodium, 45 g carbo., 4 g fiber, 30 g pro.

Salmon with Feta and Pasta

The juice in most tomatoes can dilute the flavors of the other ingredients. Because dense and meaty roma tomatoes contain less juice, they are the best choice for this colorful recipe.

1 Thaw fish, if frozen. Rinse fish; pat dry with paper towels. Cut fish in 1-inch pieces; lightly season with salt. Set aside.

2 Cook pasta according to package directions. Drain. Return pasta to hot pan; cover and keep warm.

3 Meanwhile, lightly coat a nonstick skillet with cooking spray; heat skillet over medium-high heat. Add garlic. Cook and stir for 15 seconds. Add fish to skillet. Cook fish for 4 to 6 minutes or until fish begins to flake easily when tested with a fork, turning fish pieces occasionally. Stir in tomatoes, green onions, olives, basil, and pepper; heat through.

4 In a bowl toss together warm pasta, olive oil, salmon mixture, and cheese. If desired, garnish with basil sprigs.

PER SERVING: 373 cal., 13 g total fat (5 g sat. fat), 56 mg chol., 443 mg sodium, 41 g carbo., 3 g fiber, 24 g pro.

START TO FINISH: 25 minutes

10 servings	ingredients	5 servings
1½ lb.	fresh or frozen skinless salmon fillet	12 oz.
	Salt	
1 lb.	dried rotini pasta	8 oz.
	Nonstick cooking spray	
4 cloves	garlic, minced	2 cloves
4 cups	chopped roma tomatoes	2 cups
2 cups	sliced green onions	1 cup
⅔ cup	sliced pitted ripe olives	⅓ cup
⅓ cup	snipped fresh basil	3 Tbsp.
1 tsp.	coarsely ground black pepper	½ tsp.
4 tsp.	olive oil	2 tsp.
2 4-oz. pkg.	crumbled feta cheese	1 4-oz. pkg.
	Fresh basil sprigs (optional)	

Catfish with Summer Succotash Salad

U.S. farmed catfish—raised in ponds with circulating water and fed a vegetarian diet—is one of the most environmentally friendly and sustainable seafood choices.

1 Thaw fish, if frozen. Rinse fish; pat dry with paper towels. Brush fish with olive oil and sprinkle with garlic salt and pepper; set aside.

2 Cook lima beans according to package directions. Place beans in a colander and cool quickly by running under cold water; drain. Set aside.

3 Place fish in a well-greased grill basket. For a charcoal grill, place grill basket on grill rack directly over medium coals. Grill for 6 to 9 minutes or until fish begins to flake easily when tested with a fork, turning basket once halfway through grilling. (For a gas grill, preheat grill. Reduce heat to medium. Place grill basket on grill rack directly over heat; cover and grill as above.)

4 To serve, place fish on serving platter. In a bowl toss together cooked lima beans, corn relish, and spinach. Serve with fish.

PER SERVING: 372 cal., 12 g total fat (3 g sat. fat), 53 mg chol., 509 mg sodium, 41 g carbo., 5 g fiber, 24 g pro.

PREP: 20 minutes
GRILL: 6 minutes

8 servings	ingredients	*4* servings
8 4- to 6-oz.	fresh or frozen skinless catfish fillets, about 1/2 inch thick	4 4- to 6-oz.
	Olive oil	
	Garlic salt	
	Ground black pepper	
4 cups	frozen lima beans	2 cups
2 cups	corn relish	1 cup
2 cups	fresh baby spinach	1 cup

Caribbean Crab Wraps

Call upon these festive wraps whenever sandwich boredom sets in—they're guaranteed to enliven the palate.

START TO FINISH: 25 minutes

6 servings	ingredients	3 servings
2 8-oz. pkg.	chunk-style imitation crabmeat, flaked	1 8-oz. pkg.
2 medium	zucchini, shredded	1 medium
2 cups	coarsely chopped pineapple	1 cup
1/4 cup	chopped green onions	2 Tbsp.
1/4 cup	canned diced green chile peppers	2 Tbsp.
1 tsp.	salt	1/2 tsp.
1/2 tsp.	ground black pepper	1/4 tsp.
3/4 cup	tub-style cream cheese spread with chive and onion	6 Tbsp.
6 10-inch	tomato-flavor flour tortillas	3 10-inch
2/3 cup	shredded coconut, toasted	1/3 cup

1 In a bowl toss together crabmeat, zucchini, pineapple, green onions, chile peppers, salt, and black pepper. Set aside.

2 To assemble, spread 2 tablespoons cream cheese on one side of each tortilla. Scoop/spoon some of the crabmeat mixture on the cream cheese. Sprinkle with some coconut. Roll up each wrap. Serve immediately.

PER SERVING: 386 cal., 18 g total fat (11 g sat. fat), 45 mg chol., 1,591 mg sodium, 49 g carbo., 15 g fiber, 17 g pro.

Crab and Spinach Pasta with Fontina

Get to know Fontina. Its mild, buttery, and slightly nutty taste makes it the perfect cheese for most any use. This cheese has excellent meltability.

PREP: 20 minutes   BAKE: 30 minutes
STAND: 10 minutes   OVEN: 375°F

12 servings	ingredients	6 servings
1 lb.	dried bow tie pasta	8 oz.
2 10-oz. pkg.	frozen chopped spinach, thawed and drained well	1 10-oz. pkg.
4 6- to 6.5-oz. cans	crabmeat, drained, flaked, and cartilage removed	2 6- to 6.5-oz. cans
2 26-oz. jars	pasta sauce	1 26-oz. jar
3 cups	shredded fontina cheese	1½ cups

1 Preheat oven to 375°F. Cook pasta according to package directions. Drain. Return pasta to hot pan; cover and keep warm. Meanwhile, in a bowl combine spinach and crabmeat.

2 For 12 servings, cover bottom of a 3-quart rectangular baking dish with 2 cups of the sauce. Top with pasta. Evenly top pasta with crab mixture. Sprinkle with half the cheese. Top with remaining sauce. Sprinkle remaining cheese.

3 Bake, uncovered, for 30 to 35 minutes or until sauce is bubbly around edges and cheese is slightly golden. Let stand for 10 minutes before serving.

For 6 servings: Prepare using method above, except cover bottom of a 2-quart square baking dish with 1 cup of the sauce. Top with pasta. Evenly top pasta with crab mixture. Sprinkle with half the cheese. Top with remaining sauce. Sprinkle remaining cheese.

PER SERVING: 376 cal., 11 g total fat (6 g sat. fat), 83 mg chol., 1,061 mg sodium, 45 g carbo., 5 g fiber, 27 g pro.

Macaroni and Brie with Crab

This is definitely not your everyday mac and cheese. Prepare this luxuriously rich, definitely decadent dish only when you need to dive into indulgence.

1 Preheat oven to 350°F. For 8 servings, lightly coat eight 14- to 16-ounce individual baking dishes with cooking spray; set aside. In a skillet cook onion in hot butter over medium-low heat for 15 to 20 minutes or until very tender and golden brown, stirring occasionally.

2 Meanwhile, cook pasta according to package directions. Drain. Return pasta to hot pan; cover and keep warm.

3 For sauce, add flour, salt, and pepper to onion in skillet; cook and stir about 1 minute or until combined. Add milk all at once. Cook and stir until slightly thickened and bubbly. Gradually add the chopped cheese; cook and stir over medium-low heat until cheese is melted. Stir into warm pasta; toss lightly to combine. Gently fold in crab. Transfer crab mixture to baking dishes.

4 Place bread pieces in food processor; cover and process to coarse crumbs. Sprinkle crumbs over pasta mixture.

5 Bake, uncovered, for 20 to 25 minutes or until heated through and crumbs are golden brown. If desired, add a small wedge of Brie to each dish the last 5 minutes of baking time.

For 4 servings: Prepare using method above, except lightly coat four 14- to 16-ounce individual baking dishes with cooking spray; set aside.

PER SERVING: 595 cal., 27 g total fat (16 g sat. fat), 137 mg chol., 905 mg sodium, 57 g carbo., 2 g fiber, 31 g pro.

PREP: 30 minutes   BAKE: 20 minutes
OVEN: 350°F

8 servings	ingredients	4 servings
	Nonstick cooking spray	
1 medium	sweet onion, halved and thinly sliced	½ medium
¼ cup	butter	2 Tbsp.
1 lb.	dried medium shell pasta	8 oz.
⅓ cup	all-purpose flour	3 Tbsp.
¾ tsp.	salt	½ tsp.
½ tsp.	ground black pepper	¼ tsp.
3 cups	milk	1½ cups
1 lb.	Brie cheese, trimmed and chopped (set aside small wedges for garnish)	8 oz.
2 6- to 6.5-oz. cans	crabmeat, drained, flaked, and cartilage removed	1 6- to 6.5-oz. can
3 slices	firm white bread, torn into large pieces	1½ slices

Basil-Lemon Shrimp Linguine

This light and lovely linguine looks as fresh and promising as the first day of spring—and at a mere 330 calories per serving, it will help keep you in shape for summer.

1 Thaw shrimp, if frozen. Peel and devein shrimp, leaving tails intact if desired. Rinse shrimp; pat dry with paper towels; set aside.

2 Cook pasta according to package directions, adding asparagus during the last 3 minutes of cooking. Drain. Return pasta mixture to hot pan; cover and keep warm.

3 Meanwhile, lightly coat a nonstick skillet with cooking spray; heat over medium heat. Add garlic. Cook and stir for 15 seconds. Add pepper strips. Cook and stir for 2 minutes or until crisp-tender. Add shrimp, lemon peel, salt, and black pepper. Cook and stir for 3 minutes or until shrimp are opaque. Remove from heat.

4 Add shrimp mixture to warm pasta mixture. Add snipped fresh basil, the green onions, lemon juice, and oil; toss gently to coat. Transfer to serving plates. If desired, garnish each serving with basil sprigs and/or lemon wedges.

PER SERVING: 336 cal., 6 g total fat (1 g sat. fat), 172 mg chol., 463 mg sodium, 39 g carbo., 4 g fiber, 31 g pro.

START TO FINISH: 30 minutes

8 servings	ingredients	4 servings
2 lb.	fresh or frozen large shrimp in shells	1 lb.
12 oz.	dried linguine or fettuccine	6 oz.
1 lb.	fresh asparagus spears, trimmed and cut diagonally into 1-inch pieces	8 oz.
	Nonstick cooking spray	
4 cloves	garlic, minced	2 cloves
2 cups	thin red, yellow, and/or green sweet pepper strips	1 cup
2 tsp.	finely shredded lemon peel	1 tsp.
½ tsp.	salt	¼ tsp.
½ tsp.	ground black pepper	¼ tsp.
½ cup	snipped fresh basil	¼ cup
½ cup	sliced green onions	¼ cup
¼ cup	lemon juice	2 Tbsp.
2 Tbsp.	olive oil	1 Tbsp.
	Fresh basil sprigs (optional)	
	Lemon wedges (optional)	

HOMETOWN FAVORITES

Chapter

5

ESSENTIAL SIDES

RECIPE FINDER

p. 139

p. 141

p. 147

p. 148

p. 151

p. 154

FOR MORE RECIPES:
Visit BHG.com/Recipes

Deviled Egg Salad, p.138

Deviled Egg Salad

Take this fresh and colorful dish to your next potluck—it will be the most popular offering on the salad table.

START TO FINISH: 30 minutes

12 servings	ingredients	6 servings
12	hard-cooked eggs	6
6 Tbsp.	mayonnaise or salad dressing	3 Tbsp.
2 Tbsp.	snipped fresh dill	1 Tbsp.
2 cloves	garlic, minced	1 clove
1/8 tsp.	bottled hot pepper sauce	5 dashes
1/4 tsp.	salt	1/8 tsp.
2/3 cup	olive oil	1/3 cup
1/4 cup	tarragon vinegar	2 Tbsp.
2 Tbsp.	snipped fresh dill	1 Tbsp.
4 tsp.	Dijon-style mustard	2 tsp.
2 cloves	garlic, minced	1 clove
1/2 tsp.	salt	1/4 tsp.
1/2 tsp.	bottled hot pepper sauce	1/4 tsp.
12 cups	torn Boston or Bibb lettuce	6 cups
4 cups	grape or cherry tomatoes, halved if desired	2 cups
1 1/2 cups	chopped red sweet peppers	3/4 cup
8 slices	bacon, crisp-cooked, drained, and crumbled	4 slices
6	green onions, sliced	3

1 Remove shells and halve hard-cooked eggs lengthwise; remove yolks. Set aside whites. Place yolks in a bowl; mash with a fork. For 12 servings, add mayonnaise, the 2 tablespoons snipped dill, the 2 cloves minced garlic, the 1/8 teaspoon hot pepper sauce, and the 1/4 teaspoon salt. Spoon yolk mixture into egg white halves. Set aside.

2 For vinaigrette, in a screw-top jar combine olive oil, vinegar, the 2 tablespoons snipped dill, the Dijon-style mustard, the 2 cloves minced garlic, the 1/2 teaspoon salt, and the 1/2 teaspoon bottled hot pepper sauce. Cover and shake well. Set aside.

3 To serve, use two large serving platters. On each platter arrange half the lettuce, tomatoes, sweet peppers, bacon, and green onions. Arrange half the stuffed eggs on each salad. Shake vinaigrette and drizzle on the salads.

For 6 servings: Prepare using method above, except add 3 tablespoons mayonnaise, the 1 tablespoon snipped dill, the 1 clove minced garlic, the 5 dashes hot pepper sauce, and the 1/8 teaspoon salt to mashed yolks.

For vinaigrette, in a screw-top jar combine olive oil, vinegar, the 1 tablespoon snipped dill, the Dijon-style mustard, the 1 clove minced garlic, the 1/4 teaspoon salt, and the 1/4 teaspoon bottled hot pepper sauce.

To serve, on a large serving platter arrange lettuce, tomatoes, sweet peppers, bacon, and green onions.

PER SERVING: 269 cal., 22 g total fat (4 g sat. fat), 254 mg chol., 427 mg sodium, 8 g carbo., 2 g fiber, 11 g pro.

Apple-Rice Salad

Hearty grains of brown and wild rices complement crisp apples, crunchy celery, and sunflower seeds for a healthful autumn salad. Add leftover turkey or chicken cubes to make it a main dish.

1 In a saucepan bring the water to boiling. Add brown rice and wild rice. Return to boiling; reduce heat. Simmer, covered, for 40 to 45 minutes or until rice is tender. Drain. Transfer to a bowl; cover and refrigerate for 2 hours.

2 Add apples, celery, sunflower seeds, and currants to the chilled rice mixture; stir to mix together.

3 For dressing, in a screw-top jar combine the vinegar, oil, honey, mustard, orange peel, garlic, and salt. Cover and shake well. Drizzle over rice mixture; toss lightly to coat. Serve immediately on lettuce leaves (if using). Or cover and refrigerate from 2 to 4 hours.

PER SERVING: 191 cal., 6 g total fat (1 g sat. fat), 0 mg chol., 143 mg sodium, 32 g carbo., 4 g fiber, 4 g pro.

PREP: 50 minutes
CHILL: 2 hours

12 servings	ingredients	6 servings
1¹/₂ cups	water	³/₄ cup
²/₃ cup	uncooked brown rice	¹/₃ cup
²/₃ cup	uncooked wild rice, rinsed and drained	¹/₃ cup
4 cups	chopped apples	2 cups
2 cups	thinly sliced celery	1 cup
¹/₂ cup	shelled sunflower seeds	¹/₄ cup
¹/₂ cup	dried currants or dried cranberries	¹/₄ cup
¹/₄ cup	balsamic vinegar	2 Tbsp.
2 Tbsp.	olive oil	1 Tbsp.
4 tsp.	honey	2 tsp.
4 tsp.	brown or Dijon-style mustard	2 tsp.
4 tsp.	finely shredded orange peel	2 tsp.
2 cloves	garlic, minced	1 clove
¹/₂ tsp.	salt	¹/₄ tsp.
	Lettuce leaves (optional)	

Lox-Style Pasta Salad

Lox is fresh salmon that has been brined, then either hot- or cold-smoked. A bit saltier than other varieties of smoked salmon, it has unsurpassed silky texture.

PREP: 40 minutes
CHILL: 4 hours

10 servings	ingredients	5 servings
12 oz.	dried medium shell macaroni	6 oz.
2	hard-cooked egg(s), chopped	1
1 4-oz. pkg.	thinly sliced smoked salmon (lox-style), chopped	1/2 4-oz. pkg.
1/3 cup	chopped red onion	3 Tbsp.
2 Tbsp.	capers, rinsed and drained	1 Tbsp.
1 8-oz. carton	sour cream	1/2 8-oz. carton
1/3 cup	milk	3 Tbsp.
1/4 cup	chopped fresh dill	2 Tbsp.
2 Tbsp.	mayonnaise or salad dressing	1 Tbsp.
1/2 tsp.	salt	1/4 tsp.
1/4 tsp.	freshly ground black pepper	1/8 tsp.
	Milk (optional)	

1 Cook pasta according to package directions; drain. Rinse with cold water; drain again. Transfer to a large bowl.

2 In same bowl add eggs, salmon, onion, and drained capers.

3 For dressing, in a bowl combine sour cream, the milk, dill, mayonnaise, salt, and pepper. Drizzle over pasta mixture; toss lightly to coat. Cover and refrigerator for 4 to 24 hours. Before serving, if necessary, stir in additional milk to moisten.

PER SERVING: 230 cal., 9 g total fat (4 g sat. fat), 58 mg chol., 441 mg sodium, 27 g carbo., 1 g fiber, 9 g pro.

Farm-Style Green Beans

To complete almost any entrée, this bright, crisp-tender side dish is a year-round favorite.

1 Leave green beans whole or cut in 1-inch pieces. In a saucepan cook the beans in a small amount of boiling lightly salted water about 10 minutes or until crisp-tender; drain and keep warm.

2 Meanwhile, in a skillet cook bacon over medium heat until crisp. Remove bacon; reserving drippings. Drain bacon on paper towels; set aside.

3 Cook onions and mushrooms in the reserved drippings over medium heat until tender. Add tomatoes and salt. Cook, uncovered, 2 to 3 minutes or until most of the liquid has evaporated.

4 Transfer warm green beans to a serving bowl. Top beans with onion mixture and bacon.

PER SERVING: 132 cal., 9 g total fat (3 g sat. fat), 13 mg chol., 312 mg sodium, 10 g carbo., 3 g fiber, 4 g pro.

START TO FINISH: 25 minutes

8 servings	ingredients	4 servings
1 lb.	fresh green beans, trimmed	8 oz.
4 slices	bacon, diced	2 slices
2 cups	thinly sliced onions	1 cup
1 cup	fresh sliced mushrooms	1/2 cup
3 cups	chopped tomatoes	1 1/2 cups
1/2 tsp.	salt	1/4 tsp.

Autumn Vegetable Pilaf

When sweet root vegetables marry with tender zucchini and fluffy rice, the result is a comforting cool-weather concoction.

PREP: 15 minutes
ROAST: 15 minutes
OVEN: 400°F

12 servings	ingredients	6 servings
2 6- to 7.2-oz. pkg.	rice pilaf mix	1 6- to 7.2-oz. pkg.
¼ cup	olive oil	2 Tbsp.
4 cloves	garlic, minced	2 cloves
2 tsp.	dried thyme, crushed	1 tsp.
2 cups	peeled and cubed sweet potatoes or carrots	1 cup
2 medium	zucchini, halved lengthwise and cut in ½-inch pieces	1 medium
2 small	red onion, cut in thin wedges	1 small
⅔ cup	chopped pecans or walnuts, toasted	⅓ cup
2 Tbsp.	cider vinegar	1 Tbsp.

1 Preheat oven to 400°F. Cook rice mix according to package directions, except omit butter or oil; keep warm.

2 Meanwhile, in a bowl stir together the oil, garlic, and thyme. Add sweet potatoes, zucchini, and onion, stirring to coat. Spread vegetables in a single layer in a large baking pan. Roast, uncovered, for 15 to 20 minutes or until vegetables are lightly browned and tender, stirring occasionally.

3 Stir vegetable mixture, nuts, and vinegar into warm rice. Serve immediately.

PER SERVING: 244 cal., 9 g total fat (1 g sat. fat), 0 mg chol., 349 mg sodium, 37 g carbo., 4 g fiber, 4 g pro.

Cheesy Brussels Sprouts with Bacon

Brussels sprouts—people either love them or they don't. Those who love them will adore this dish—and those who don't may change their minds once they taste its creamy-rich goodness.

PREP: 15 minutes   BAKE: 20 minutes
OVEN: 400°F

8 servings	ingredients	4 servings
8 cups	Brussels sprouts, quartered	4 cups
3 slices	bacon, diced	1½ slices
½ cup	chopped onion	¼ cup
2 cloves	garlic, minced	1 clove
1 16-oz. jar	Alfredo or white pasta sauce	½ 16-oz. jar
1 cup	soft bread crumbs	½ cup
⅓ cup	shredded Parmesan cheese	3 Tbsp.
2 Tbsp.	butter, melted	1 Tbsp.

1 Preheat oven to 400°F. Cook Brussels sprouts in a small amount of lightly salted boiling water for 5 minutes (sprouts will not be tender); drain and keep warm.

2 Meanwhile, in an oven-going skillet cook bacon over medium heat until crisp; remove bacon, reserving drippings. Drain bacon on paper towels; set aside.

3 Add onion and garlic to skillet; cook until onion is tender. In skillet combine Brussels sprouts, bacon, onion mixture, and Alfredo sauce. Toss lightly to coat.

4 In a bowl combine bread crumbs, Parmesan cheese, and melted butter. Sprinkle over Brussels sprouts mixture.

5 Bake, uncovered, for 20 to 25 minutes or until heated through and topping is golden.

PER SERVING: 309 cal., 22 g total fat (10 g sat. fat), 51 mg chol., 817 mg sodium, 15 g carbo., 4 g fiber, 14 g pro.

Cheesy Garlic Potato Gratin

Any chop, roast, or steak is even better with a great potato side dish. This one—rich with cheese and garlic—is one of the best.

1 Preheat oven to 350°F. For 12 servings, grease a 3-quart rectangular baking dish. Layer half the sliced potatoes and half the green onions in the prepared dish. Sprinkle with half the garlic, salt, pepper, and cheese. Repeat layers. Pour whipping cream over top.

2 Bake, covered, for 1¼ hours. Uncover and bake for 15 to 25 minutes more or until potatoes are tender when pierced with a fork and top is golden brown. Let stand for 10 minutes before serving.

For 6 servings: Prepare using method above, except grease a 2-quart square baking dish.

PER SERVING: 349 cal., 24 g total fat (15 g sat. fat). 85 mg chol., 470 mg sodium, 21 g carbo., 2 g fiber, 13 g pro.

PREP: 20 minutes COOK: 1½ hours
STAND: 10 minutes OVEN: 350°F

12 servings	ingredients	6 servings
10 cups	thinly sliced Yukon gold or other yellow-flesh potatoes	5 cups
⅔ cup	sliced green onions	⅓ cup
4 tsp.	minced garlic	2 tsp.
2 tsp.	salt	1 tsp.
½ tsp.	ground black pepper	¼ tsp.
3 cups	shredded Swiss cheese, provolone, or Jarlsberg cheese	1½ cups
2 cups	whipping cream	1 cup

Creamed Corn Casserole

Serve this family-friendly favorite to brighten the table any weeknight. Corn dishes are favorites for almost anyone

PREP: 15 minutes
BAKE: 45 minutes
STAND: 5 minutes
OVEN: 375°F

1 Preheat oven to 375°F. For 12 servings, lightly coat a 2-quart casserole with cooking spray; set aside. Place corn in a colander and thaw under cold running water; drain. Set aside.

2 In a large saucepan cook sweet peppers and onion in hot butter over medium heat until tender. Stir in drained corn and black pepper. In a bowl whisk together soup, cream cheese spread, and milk. Stir soup mixture into corn mixture. Transfer to prepared casserole.

3 Bake, covered, for 45 to 55 minutes or until heated through, stirring once. Let stand for 5 minutes before serving.

For 6 servings: Prepare using method above, except lightly coat a 1-quart casserole with cooking spray; set aside.

PER SERVING: 176 cal., 9 g total fat (5 g sat. fat), 22 mg chol., 280 mg sodium, 22 g carbo., 3 g fiber, 4 g pro.

12 servings	ingredients	6 servings
	Nonstick cooking spray	
2 16-oz. pkg.	frozen whole kernel corn	1 16-oz. pkg.
2 cups	chopped red and/or green sweet peppers	1 cup
1 cup	chopped onion	½ cup
1 Tbsp.	butter or margarine	1½ tsp.
¼ tsp.	ground black pepper	⅛ tsp.
1 10.75-oz. can	condensed cream of celery soup	½ 10.75-oz. can
1 8-oz. tub	cream cheese spread with chive and onion or cream cheese spread with garden vegetables	½ 8-oz. tub
¼ cup	milk	2 Tbsp.

Garlic and Pepper Stir-Fry

Nutty-flavor sesame oil has a high smoke point, which makes it excellent for high-heat stir-frying. Choose a light-color toasted sesame oil for this light and tasty side dish.

START TO FINISH: 25 minutes

8 servings	ingredients	4 servings
¼ cup	soy sauce	2 Tbsp.
2 tsp.	toasted sesame oil	1 tsp.
½ tsp.	cracked black pepper	¼ tsp.
2 Tbsp.	vegetable oil	1 Tbsp.
6 cloves	garlic, minced	3 cloves
4 medium	red, yellow, and/or green sweet peppers, cut in bite-size strips	2 medium
2 medium	onion(s), sliced and separated in rings	1 medium
4 cups	sliced fresh mushrooms	2 cups
	Toasted sesame seeds	

1 For sauce, in a bowl combine soy sauce, sesame oil, and black pepper; set aside.

2 Pour oil into a large wok or an extra-large skillet; heat wok over medium-high heat. (Add more oil as necessary during cooking.) Add garlic; cook and stir for 1 minute. Add sweet peppers and onion rings; cook and stir for 3 minutes. Add mushrooms; cook and stir for 2 to 3 minutes more or until vegetables are crisp-tender.

3 Push vegetables from center to side of wok. Stir sauce; add to wok. Cook and stir until bubbly; combine with vegetables until vegetables are coated. Transfer to a serving dish. Sprinkle with sesame seeds. Serve immediately.

PER SERVING: 95 cal., 6 g total fat (1 g sat. fat), 0 mg chol., 464 mg sodium, 8 g carbo., 2 g fiber, 4 g pro.

Herbed Leek Gratin

Leeks practically melt into the marjoram-spiked sauce of this luxurious, subtly sweet side dish. It is super alongside roasted chicken—and can bake in the oven at the same time.

1 Preheat oven to 375°F. Trim roots from leeks, leaving pieces 4 to 5 inches long with white and pale green parts. Cut leeks in half lengthwise. Thoroughly rinse leeks under cold running water; pat dry with paper towels. For 9 servings, arrange leeks, cut sides down, in a greased 3-quart rectangular baking dish, overlapping leeks to fit. (Leeks should all face the same direction.)

2 In a bowl combine whipping cream and chicken broth; pour over leeks. Sprinkle with half the marjoram, the salt, and pepper. Bake, covered, for 20 minutes.

3 Meanwhile, in a bowl combine bread crumbs, Parmesan cheese, and remaining marjoram. Drizzle with melted butter; toss lightly to coat. Sprinkle bread crumb mixture over leeks.

4 Bake, uncovered, for 15 to 20 minutes more or until leeks are tender and crumbs are golden brown. If desired, garnish with fresh marjoram sprigs.

For 6 servings: Prepare using method above, except arrange leeks, cut sides down, in a greased 2-quart rectangular baking dish, overlapping leeks to fit.

PER SERVING: 237 cal., 15 g total fat (9 g sat. fat), 46 mg chol., 476 mg sodium, 23 g carbo., 2 g fiber, 4 g pro.

PREP: 15 minutes
BAKE: 35 minutes
OVEN: 375°F

9 servings	ingredients	6 servings
4½ lb.	slender leeks	3 lb.
¾ cup	whipping cream	½ cup
¾ cup	chicken broth	½ cup
3 Tbsp.	snipped fresh marjoram	2 Tbsp.
¾ tsp.	salt	½ tsp.
¾ tsp.	freshly ground black pepper	½ tsp.
2¼ cups	soft French or Italian bread crumbs	1½ cups
⅓ Tbsp.	grated Parmesan cheese	3 Tbsp.
⅓ Tbsp.	butter, melted	3 Tbsp.
	Fresh marjoram sprigs (optional)	

Broccoli-Cauliflower Bake

Cruciferous vegetables such as broccoli and cauliflower are packed with antioxidants and are high in fiber, vitamins, and minerals too.

PREP: 20 minutes
BAKE: 20 minutes
OVEN: 375°F

1 Preheat oven to 375°F. Cook broccoli and cauliflower, covered, in a small amount of boiling lightly salted water for 6 to 8 minutes or until vegetables are almost crisp-tender; drain. Remove broccoli and cauliflower from pan; set aside.

2 For 8 servings, in the same saucepan cook onion in the 1 tablespoon hot butter over medium heat until tender, stirring occasionally. Stir in soup, cheese, milk, and basil. Cook and stir over medium-low heat until bubbly and cheese is melted. Gently stir in broccoli and cauliflower. Transfer mixture to a 2-quart casserole. In a bowl toss together bread crumbs and the 1 tablespoon melted butter; sprinkle over vegetable mixture.

3 Bake, uncovered, about 20 minutes or until heated through.

For 4 servings: Prepare using method above, except in Step 2 transfer mixture to a 1-quart casserole and mix bread crumbs with 1¹/₂ teaspoons melted butter.

PER SERVING: 141 cal., 9 g total fat (4 g sat. fat), 19 mg chol., 506 mg sodium, 11 g carbo., 3 g fiber, 5 g pro.

8 servings	ingredients	4 servings
4 cups	broccoli florets	2 cups
3 cups	cauliflower florets	1¹/₂ cups
¹/₂ cup	chopped onion	¹/₄ cup
1 Tbsp.	butter or margarine	1¹/₂ tsp.
1 10.75-oz. can	condensed cream of mushroom soup or cream of chicken soup	¹/₂ 10.75-oz. can
3 oz.	American cheese or process Swiss cheese, torn	1¹/₂ oz.
¹/₄ cup	milk	2 Tbsp.
¹/₂ tsp.	dried basil, thyme, or marjoram, crushed	¹/₄ tsp.
1 cup	soft bread crumbs	¹/₂ cup
1 Tbsp.	butter or margarine, melted	1¹/₂ tsp.

Baked Butter Beans with Mustard

In the southern U.S., large dried lima beans, or Fordhook beans, are often referred to as butter beans.

PREP: 20 minutes   BAKE: 45 minutes
OVEN: 325°F

10 servings	ingredients	5 servings
8 slices	bacon, diced	4 slices
1 cup	chopped onion	1/2 cup
4 16-oz. cans	butter beans and/or Great Northern beans, rinsed and drained	2 16-oz. cans
1 8-oz. carton	sour cream	1/8-oz. carton
1/2 cup	chicken or vegetable broth	1/4 cup
1 Tbsp.	all-purpose flour	1 1/2 tsp.
1 Tbsp.	snipped fresh rosemary	1 1/2 tsp.
1 Tbsp.	Dijon-style mustard	1 1/2 tsp.
1/2 tsp.	freshly ground black pepper	1/4 tsp.
2 Tbsp.	chopped Italian (flat-leaf) parsley	1 Tbsp.
2 tsp.	finely shredded lemon peel	1 tsp.

1 Preheat oven to 325°F. In a skillet cook bacon over medium heat until crisp; remove bacon, reserving 1 tablespoon drippings. Drain bacon on paper towels; set aside. Cook onion in reserved drippings over medium heat until tender. Transfer onion to a bowl. Add drained beans and all but 2 tablespoons of the bacon; set aside.

2 In another bowl whisk together sour cream, broth, flour, rosemary, mustard, and pepper. Stir into bean mixture. For 10 servings, transfer to a 2-quart casserole.

3 Bake, covered, for 45 minutes, stirring once halfway through. In a bowl combine remaining bacon, the parsley, and lemon peel; sprinkle on beans just before serving.

For 5 servings: Prepare using method above, except transfer to a 1-quart casserole.

PER SERVING: 247 cal., 10 g total fat (5 g sat. fat), 20 mg chol., 892 mg sodium, 26 g carbo., 6 g fiber, 12 g pro.

Focaccia Breadsticks

With refrigerated pizza dough, these enticing twists are amazingly easy to make. Serve them with pasta dishes or alongside minestrone, cheese, and vegetable soups.

1 Preheat oven to 350°F. For 20 servings, lightly grease two large baking sheets; set aside. Drain dried tomatoes, reserving 4 teaspoons of the oil. Finely snip tomatoes. In a bowl combine tomatoes, cheese, rosemary, pepper, the reserved oil, and the water. Set aside.

2 Unroll pizza dough. On a lightly floured surface roll each dough portion in a 10×8-inch rectangle. Spread the tomato mixture crosswise over half each rectangle.

3 Fold plain dough half over filling; press lightly to seal edges. Cut each folded dough rectangle lengthwise into ten 1/2-inch-wide strips about 8 inches long. Fold each strip in half and twist two or three times. Place 1 inch apart on the prepared baking sheets.

4 Bake for 12 to 15 minutes or until golden. Immediately remove rolls from pans. Serve warm.

For 10 servings: Prepare using method above, except lightly grease a large baking sheet; set aside. Drain dried tomatoes, reserving 2 teaspoons of the oil.

PER SERVING: 84 cal., 2 g total fat (1 g sat. fat), 2 mg chol., 209 mg sodium, 14 g carbo., 1 g fiber, 3 g pro.

PREP: 20 mintues
BAKE: 12 minutes
OVEN: 350°F

20 servings	ingredients	10 servings
1/2 cup	oil-packed dried tomatoes	1/4 cup
1/2 cup	grated Parmesan or Romano cheese	1/4 cup
2 tsp.	snipped fresh rosemary, crushed	1 tsp.
1/4 tsp.	cracked black pepper	1/8 tsp.
4 tsp.	water	2 tsp.
2 10-oz. pkg.	refrigerated pizza dough	1 10-oz. pkg.

Cheddar-Corn Bread Rolls

Amaze your family by bringing a basket of homemade rolls to the table. This recipe makes it possible. These fluffy, cheese-studded rolls take less than an hour from start to finish.

**PREP: 10 minutes   RISE: 20 minutes   BAKE: 20 minutes
STAND: 5 minutes   OVEN: 375°F**

30 servings	ingredients	15 servings
2 16-oz. pkg.	hot roll mix	1 16-oz. pkg.
2 cups	shredded cheddar cheese	1 cup
²/₃ cup	cornmeal	¹/₃ cup
2¹/₂ cups	hot water (120°F to 130°F)	1¹/₄ cups
¹/₄ cup	olive oil	2 Tbsp.
2	egg(s), lightly beaten	1
	Milk	
	Cornmeal	

1 For 30 servings, in a bowl combine flour from the hot roll mixes, the contents of the yeast packets, the cheese, and the ²/₃ cup cornmeal. Add the hot water, oil, and egg(s); stir until combined.

2 Turn out dough onto a well-floured surface. Knead dough for 5 minutes or until smooth and elastic. Divide in half. Cover and let rest for 5 minutes. Lightly grease two 13×9×2-inch baking pans or baking sheets; set aside.

3 Divide each dough portion in 15 pieces. Shape each piece in a ball by pulling and tucking the dough underneath. Arrange 15 balls in each prepared pan. Cover and let rise in a warm place for 20 minutes.

4 Preheat oven to 375°F. Brush dough with milk and sprinkle with additional cornmeal. Bake, one pan at a time, for 20 to 22 minutes or until golden. Immediately remove rolls from pans. Cool on wire racks.

For 15 servings: Prepare using method above, except lightly grease one 13×9×2-inch baking pan; set aside.

PER SERVING: 176 cal., 5 g total fat (2 g sat. fat), 22 mg chol., 228 mg sodium, 26 g carbo., 0 g fiber, 7 g pro.

HOMETOWN FAVORITES

Chapter

6

MOST-REQUESTED DESSERTS

RECIPE FINDER

p. 160

p. 164

p. 174

p. 177

p. 178

p. 185

FOR MORE RECIPES:
Visit BHG.com/Recipes

Banana Split Cake, p. 176

Lime Zingers

Butter—lots of it—makes these zesty shortbread rounds utterly rich, tender, and delectable.

PREP: 40 minutes   BAKE: 8 minutes per batch
OVEN: 350°F

84 cookies	ingredients	42 cookies
2 cups	butter, softened	1 cup
1 cup	granulated sugar	½ cup
4 tsp.	finely shredded lime peel	2 tsp.
½ cup	lime juice	¼ cup
2 tsp.	vanilla	1 tsp.
4½ cups	all-purpose flour	2¼ cups
1½ cups	finely chopped Brazil nuts or hazelnuts (filberts)	¾ cup
1 8-oz. pkg.	cream cheese, softened	½ 8-oz. pkg.
2 cups	powdered sugar	1 cup
2 Tbsp.	lime juice	1 Tbsp.
2 tsp.	vanilla	1 tsp.
	Finely shredded lime peel (optional)	

1 Preheat oven to 350°F. For 84 cookies, in a mixing bowl beat butter with an electric mixer on medium to high speed for 30 seconds. Add the granulated sugar. Beat until combined, scraping sides of bowl occasionally. Beat in the 4 teaspoons lime peel, ½ cup lime juice, and 2 teaspoons vanilla until combined. Beat in as much of the flour as you can with the mixer. Using a wooden spoon, stir in any remaining flour and the nuts. Divide dough in fourths.

2 On a lightly floured surface, roll one-fourth of the dough at a time to ¼-inch thickness, rolling from the center and pushing dough toward the edges to uniform thickness. Cut dough in rounds using a 2-inch cookie cutter. Place cutouts 1 inch apart on ungreased cookie sheets.

3 Bake for 8 to 10 minutes or until edges are light brown. Transfer to a wire rack to cool.

4 For frosting, in a mixing bowl combine cream cheese, powdered sugar, the 2 tablespoons lime juice, and 2 teaspoons vanilla. Beat with an electric mixer on medium speed until smooth. Spread frosting on cooled cookies. If desired, sprinkle with additional lime peel.

For 42 cookies: Prepare using method above, except in Step divide dough in half.

PER COOKIE: 62 cal., 4 g total fat (2 g sat. fat), 9 mg chol., 31 mg sodium, 6 g carbo., 0 g fiber, 1 g pro.

Frosted Walnut Cookies

Shelled walnuts should be plump, meaty, and crisp. To keep nuts at their prime, store them, tightly covered, in the refrigerator up to 6 months.

1 Preheat oven to 375°F. Grease a cookie sheet; set aside.

2 For 60 cookies, in a large mixing bowl beat shortening with an electric mixer on medium speed for 30 seconds. Add brown sugar, baking soda, baking powder, and salt. Beat until combined, scraping sides of bowl occasionally. Beat in eggs and the 1 teaspoon vanilla until combined. Alternately add flour and sour cream to sugar mixture, beating until combined after each addition. Stir in the ²/₃ cup nuts.

3 Drop dough by rounded teaspoons 2 inches apart onto the prepared cookie sheet. Bake for 10 to 12 minutes or until edges are light brown. Transfer to a wire rack to cool.

4 For frosting, in a mixing bowl beat butter with 2 cups of the powdered sugar. Beat in milk and 1¹/₂ teaspoons vanilla until smooth. Gradually beat in the remaining 2 cups powdered sugar. If necessary, beat in additional milk to make spreading consistency.

5 Spread frosting on cooled cookies. If desired, top with additional walnuts.

For 30 cookies: Prepare using method above, except beat in eggs and the ¹/₂ teaspoon vanilla until combined. Stir in the ¹/₃ cup nuts.

For frosting, in a mixing bowl beat butter with 1 cup of the powdered sugar. Beat in milk and ³/₄ teaspoon vanilla until smooth. Gradually beat in the remaining 1 cup powdered sugar.

PER COOKIE: 105 cal., 5 g total fat (2 g sat. fat), 13 mg chol., 63 mg sodium, 14 g carbo., 0 g fiber, 1 g pro.

PREP: 40 minutes   BAKE: 10 minutes per batch
OVEN: 375°F

60 cookies	ingredients	30 cookies
¹/₂ cup	shortening	¹/₄ cup
1¹/₂ cups	packed brown sugar	³/₄ cup
1 tsp.	baking soda	¹/₂ tsp.
¹/₂ tsp.	baking powder	¹/₄ tsp.
¹/₂ tsp.	salt	¹/₄ tsp.
2	egg(s)	1
1 tsp.	vanilla	¹/₂ tsp.
2¹/₂ cups	all-purpose flour	1¹/₄ cups
1 8-oz. carton	sour cream	¹/₂ 8-oz. carton
²/₃ cup	chopped walnuts	¹/₃ cup
¹/₃ cup	butter, softened	3 Tbsp.
4 cups	powdered sugar	2 cups
¹/₄ cup	milk	2 Tbsp.
1¹/₂ tsp.	vanilla	³/₄ tsp.
	Chopped walnuts or walnut halves (optional)	

Chocolate Dreams

These puffy domes with three chocolates and buttery-rich macadamia nuts are delightful. Serve them to your sweetheart or when you crave delicious chocolate.

PREP: 35 minutes
BAKE: 8 minutes
OVEN: 350°F

40 cookies	ingredients	20 cookies
8 oz.	bittersweet chocolate, chopped	4 oz.
2 Tbsp.	butter	1 Tbsp.
3 Tbsp.	all-purpose flour	5 tsp.
¼ tsp.	baking powder	⅛ tsp.
2	egg(s)	1
⅔ cup	sugar	⅓ cup
1 tsp.	vanilla	½ tsp.
2 cups	chopped macadamia nuts	1 cup
1½ cups	semisweet chocolate pieces	¾ cup
6 oz.	semisweet chocolate (optional)	4 oz.
1½ tsp.	shortening (optional)	1 tsp.

1 In a saucepan cook and stir bittersweet chocolate and butter over low heat until melted and smooth. Remove pan from heat and cool about 20 minutes.

2 Preheat oven to 350°F. Line two large cookie sheets with foil or parchment paper; set aside.

3 In a bowl combine flour and baking powder; set aside. In a mixing bowl beat egg(s), sugar, and vanilla with an electric mixer on medium speed about 5 minutes or until mixture is thickened and pale yellow. Gently stir in flour mixture and cooled chocolate. Gently stir in nuts and chocolate pieces.

4 Immediately, using a small cookie scoop (1½ inches in diameter), drop dough in mounds 1 inch apart on prepared cookie sheets. (Dough will thicken as it stands.)

5 Bake both sheets of cookies at the same time on separate racks for 8 to 9 minutes or until edges are set but centers are soft, reversing sheets to opposite racks halfway through baking. Completely cool cookies on sheets on wire racks. Peel cooled cookies off the foil or parchment paper.

6 For drizzle, in a small saucepan melt chocolate and shortening over low heat, stirring often. Drizzle melted chocolate over tops in a criss-cross pattern.

PER COOKIE: 132 cal., 10 g total fat (4 g sat. fat), 12 mg chol., 11 mg sodium, 12 g carbo., 1 g fiber, 1 g pro.

Butterscotch Brownies

These buttery bars have the old-fashioned flavor of butterscotch combined with chunky nuts and melt-in-the-mouth marshmallows—for magnificent results.

PREP: 20 minutes   BAKE: 15 minutes
COOL: 20 minutes   OVEN: 350°F

24 bars	ingredients	12 bars
¹/₃ cup	butter	3 Tbsp.
²/₃ cup	coconut	¹/₃ cup
³/₄ cup	chopped pecans	¹/₃ cup
²/₃ cup	packed brown sugar	¹/₃ cup
¹/₂ cup	butter, softened	¹/₄ cup
1 cup	packed brown sugar	¹/₂ cup
¹/₂ tsp.	baking soda	¹/₄ tsp.
¹/₄ tsp.	salt	¹/₈ tsp.
3	egg(s)	1
¹/₂ tsp.	vanilla	¹/₄ tsp.
1¹/₂ cups	all-purpose flour	³/₄ cup
¹/₂ cup	chopped pecans	¹/₄ cup
¹/₂ cup	tiny marshmallows	¹/₄ cup
	Caramel-flavor ice cream topping (optional)	

1 Preheat oven to 350°F. For 24 bars, grease a 13×9×2-inch baking pan; set aside. In a saucepan melt the ¹/₃ cup butter; stir in coconut, the ³/₄ cup pecans, and the ²/₃ cup brown sugar. Press evenly in prepared pan; set aside.

2 In a mixing bowl beat the ¹/₂ cup butter with an electric mixer on medium to high speed for 30 seconds. Add the 1 cup brown sugar, baking soda, and salt. Beat until combined, scraping sides of bowl occasionally. Beat in eggs and vanilla until combined. Add flour and beat until combined. Stir in the ¹/₂ cup pecans and marshmallows. Spoon small mounds of mixture on coconut mixture in pan. Carefully spread to cover.

3 Bake for 15 to 20 minutes (mixture should be evenly browned; center may jiggle slightly when gently shaken). Cool in pan on a wire rack for 20 minutes.

4 To serve, cut into bars. Drizzle with caramel topping.

For 12 bars: Prepare using method above, except grease an 8×8×2-inch baking pan; set aside. In a saucepan melt the 3 tablespoons butter; stir in coconut, the ¹/₃ cup pecans, and the ¹/₃ cup brown sugar. In a mixing bowl beat ¹/₄ cup butter with an electric mixer on medium to high speed for 30 seconds. Add ¹/₂ cup brown sugar, baking soda, and salt; beat until combined. Beat in egg and vanilla until combined. Add flour and beat until combined. Stir in ¹/₄ cup pecans and marshmallows.

PER BAR: 211 cal., 13 g total fat (6 g sat. fat), 43 mg chol., 113 mg sodium, 23 g carbo., 1 g fiber, 2 g pro.

Oat-Rhubarb Streusel Bars

In the United States rhubarb is often paired with strawberries. In Britain it appears more often with ginger, as it does here in these crumbly English-style bars.

1 Preheat oven to 350°F. For 32 bars, line a 13×9×2-inch baking pan with heavy foil, extending foil over the sides of the pan; set aside.

2 In a bowl stir together oats, the 2 cups flour, and brown sugar. Cut in butter until mixture resembles coarse crumbs. Set aside 2 cups oats mixture. Press remaining mixture in prepared pan. Bake for 25 minutes. Remove from oven; set aside.

3 Meanwhile, in a bowl stir together granulated sugar, the ¼ cup flour, and the 1 teaspoon ground ginger. Add rhubarb; toss lightly to coat. Spread rhubarb mixture on partially baked crust. Sprinkle with reserved oats mixture; press lightly.

4 Bake for 30 to 40 minutes or until top is golden and filling is bubbly. Cool on a wire rack for 1 hour.

5 For icing, in a bowl combine powdered sugar and ½ teaspoon ginger. Stir in apricot nectar.

6 Remove bars from pan using the foil to lift out. Place on cutting board; cut into bars. Drizzle icing and sprinkle crystallized ginger on bars. Store, covered, in the refrigerator up to 2 days.

For 16 bars: Prepare using method above, except line an 8×8×2-inch baking pan with foil. In Step 2 use 1 cup flour and set aside 1 cup oats mixture. In Step 3 use 2 tablespoons flour and ½ teaspoon ginger. In Step 5 make icing using amounts suggested.

PER BAR: 221 cal., 10 g total fat (5 g sat. fat), 24 mg chol., 70 mg sodium, 32 g carbo., 1 g fiber, 2 g pro.

PREP: 20 minutes   BAKE: 55 minutes
COOL: 1 hour   OVEN: 350°F

32 bars	ingredients	16 bars
3 cups	quick-cooking rolled oats	1½ cups
2 cups	all-purpose flour	1 cup
1½ cups	packed brown sugar	¾ cup
1½ cups	butter	¾ cup
½ cup	granulated sugar	¼ cup
¼ cup	all-purpose flour	2 Tbsp.
1 tsp.	ground ginger	½ tsp.
4 cups	fresh or frozen unsweetened sliced rhubarb	2 cups
1½ cups	powdered sugar	¾ cup
½ tsp.	ground ginger	¼ tsp.
⅓ cup	apricot nectar, orange juice, or milk	3 to 4 tsp.
2 Tbsp.	finely chopped crystallized ginger (optional)	1 Tbsp.

Peanut Butter Bars

This recipe is one to introduce kids to the joy of baking. The measurements are simple, patting the bottom layer into the pan is fun, and the result will make them proud.

PREP: 20 minutes
BAKE: 30 minutes
COOL: 20 minutes
OVEN: 350°F

32 bars	ingredients	16 bars
3 cups	all-purpose flour	1½ cups
1 cup	salted peanuts, finely chopped	½ cup
1 cup	sugar	½ cup
¼ tsp.	salt	⅛ tsp.
1 cup	peanut butter	½ cup
¾ cup	butter	6 Tbsp.
2 tsp.	vanilla	1 tsp.
3 cups	tiny marshmallows	1½ cups
1 cup	semisweet chocolate pieces	½ cup

1 Preheat oven to 350°F. For 32 bars, grease a 15×10×1-inch baking pan; set aside.

2 In a bowl stir together flour, peanuts, sugar, and salt. Using a pastry blender, cut in peanut butter and butter until crumbly. Stir in vanilla. Firmly pat 6 cups of the flour mixture into bottom of prepared pan.

3 Bake for 20 minutes. Evenly top with marshmallows, chocolate pieces, and remaining crumb mixture.

4 Bake for 10 to 15 minutes more or until marshmallows are toasted and crumbs are golden. Cool in pan on a wire rack for 20 minutes. Cut in bars (bars will be slightly crumbly).

For 16 bars: Prepare using method above, except grease a 8×8×2-inch baking pan; set aside. In Step 2 firmly pat 3 cups of the flour mixture into bottom of prepared pan.

PER BAR: 221 cal., 12 g total fat (5 g sat. fat), 11 mg chol., 104 mg sodium, 23 g carbo., 2 g fiber, 5 g pro.

Super-Easy Chocolate Bars

Sweetened condensed milk in the filling for these bars is all the sweetener that's needed. These are decadently rich and satisfying.

PREP: 20 minutes   BAKE: 30 minutes   OVEN: 350°F

24 bars	ingredients	12 bars
1 cup	butter, softened	½ cup
½ cup	sugar	¼ cup
⅛ tsp.	salt	dash
2 cups	all-purpose flour	1 cup
1 14-oz. can (1¼ cups)	sweetened condensed milk	½ cup + 2 Tbsp.
1 cup	semisweet chocolate pieces	½ cup
½ cup	chopped walnuts or pecans	¼ cup
½ tsp.	vanilla	¼ tsp.

1 Preheat oven to 350°F. For crust, in a large mixing bowl beat butter with an electric mixer on medium to high speed for 30 seconds. Add sugar and salt; beat until combined, scraping sides of bowl occasionally. Beat in the flour on low speed until combined. For 24 bars, press two-thirds of the crust mixture into the bottom of an ungreased 13×9×2-inch baking pan.

2 For filling, in a medium saucepan combine sweetened condensed milk and chocolate. Stir over low heat until chocolate is melted and mixture is smooth. Remove from heat. Stir in nuts and vanilla. Spread hot chocolate mixture over the crust. Dot with remaining crust mixture.

3 Bake for 30 to 35 minutes or until golden. Cool on a wire rack. Cut into squares.

For 12 bars: Prepare using method above, except use an ungreased 8×8×2-inch baking pan.

PER BAR: 213 cal., 13 g total fat (6 g sat. fat), 26 mg chol., 87 mg sodium, 24 g carbo., 1 g fiber, 3 g pro.

Key Lime Cheesecake Bars

Fresh Key limes—small, round yellowish limes from Florida—may be hard to find, but the bottled juice or regular Persian limes are good substitutes in this fresh and zesty bar cookie.

1 Preheat oven to 350°F. For 30 bars, line two 9×9×2-inch baking pans with foil, extending foil about 1 inch over the sides of each pan. Lightly grease foil; set pans aside.

2 For crust, in a bowl combine crushed pretzels, the ¼ sugar, and the melted butter. Divide in half. Evenly press each half in each prepared baking pan. Bake for 10 minutes. Remove from oven; cool on a wire rack.

3 For filling, in a mixing bowl beat cream cheese, the 1⅓ cups sugar, and vanilla with an electric mixer until combined. Stir in eggs. Stir in lime juice and lime peel. Pour filling, dividing evenly, in each partially baked crust. Sprinkle each with pistachio nuts.

4 Bake for 20 to 30 minutes or until center appears set. Cool in pans on wire racks for 30 minutes. Cover and refrigerate for 4 to 24 hours (top will crack slightly). Remove from pans, using the overlapping foil to lift. Place on cutting board; cut into bars.

For 15 bars: Prepare using method above, except in Step use a 9×9×2-inch baking pan. In Step 2 for crust, combine crushed pretzels, the 2 tablespoons sugar, and melted butter. In Step 3 for filling, beat cream cheese, the ⅔ cup sugar, and vanilla.

PER BAR: 254 cal., 19 g total fat (11 g sat. fat), 92 mg chol., 276 mg sodium, 17 g carbo., 0 g fiber, 4 g pro.

PREP: 20 minutes   BAKE: 30 minutes   COOL: 30 minutes
CHILL: 4 hours   OVEN: 350°F

30 bars	ingredients	15 bars
2 cups	finely crushed pretzel sticks	1 cup
¼ cup	sugar	2 Tbsp.
1 cup	butter, melted	½ cup
4 8-oz. pkg.	cream cheese, softened	2 8-oz. pkg.
1⅓ cups	sugar	⅔ cup
2 tsp.	vanilla	1 tsp.
6	eggs, lightly beaten	3
⅓ cup	bottled Key lime juice or regular lime juice	3 Tbsp.
1 tsp.	finely shredded lime peel	½ tsp.
½ cup	chopped salted pistachio nuts	¼ cup

Cherry Cheesecake Bars

Maraschino cherries are the Queen Anne variety that have been macerated in almond-flavored sugar syrup. Their pretty color makes this recipe one to remember for Valentine's Day.

PREP: 25 minutes
BAKE: 30 minutes
COOL: 1 hour
CHILL: 4 hours
OVEN: 350°F

32 bars	ingredients	16 bars
2 cups (about 55 wafers)	finely crushed vanilla wafers	1 cup (about 26 wafers)
⅓ cup	butter, melted	3 Tbsp.
1 10-oz. jar	maraschino cherries	½ 10-oz. jar
2 8-oz. pkg.	cream cheese, softened	1 8-oz. pkg.
1 cup	sugar	½ cup
5	egg whites, lightly beaten	3

1 Preheat oven to 350°F. For 32 servings, line a 13×9×2-inch baking pan with foil, extending the foil about 1 inch over the sides of pan; set aside.

2 For crust, in a bowl combine crushed wafers and melted butter. Press mixture evenly in prepared pan. Bake for 10 minutes. Remove from oven; set aside.

3 Meanwhile, drain cherries well, reserving 2 tablespoons of the liquid. If necessary, remove and discard stems from cherries. Finely chop the cherries; set cherries aside.

4 In a mixing bowl beat cream cheese and sugar with an electric mixer on medium speed until combined. Beat in reserved cherry liquid until combined. Stir in egg whites and chopped cherries.

5 Pour cream cheese mixture over partially baked crust, spreading evenly. Bake for 20 to 25 minutes or until set. Cool in pan on a wire rack for 1 hour. Cover and refrigerate for 4 to 24 hours. Remove from pans, using foil to lift. Place on cutting board; cut into bars.

For 16 bars: Prepare using method above, except use a 9×9×2-inch baking pan. In Step 3 reserve 1 tablespoon of the cherry liquid.

PER BAR: 157 cal., 9 g total fat (5 g sat. fat), 21 mg chol., 96 mg sodium, 18 g carbo., 0 g fiber, 2 g pro.

White Chocolate Brownies

For the best results and superb flavor when baking with white chocolate, choose a product that lists cocoa butter in its ingredients label.

PREP: 15 minutes   BAKE: 30 minutes
COOL: 20 minutes   OVEN: 350°F

40 brownies	ingredients	20 brownies
½ cup	unsalted butter (no substitutes)	¼ cup
12 oz.	white baking chocolate, coarsely chopped	6 oz.
4	eggs	2
1 cup	sugar	½ cup
2 cups	all-purpose flour	1 cup
1 tsp.	salt	½ tsp.
1 tsp.	vanilla	½ tsp.
2 cups	semisweet chocolate pieces	1 cup

1 Preheat oven to 350°F. For 40 brownies, lightly grease a 13×9×2-inch baking pan; set aside. In a heavy saucepan heat and stir butter and half the chopped white chocolate over low heat until combined. Remove pan from heat; set aside.

2 In a mixing bowl beat eggs with an electric mixer on medium to medium-high speed until thick and foamy. Gradually add sugar and beat about 3 minutes or until thickened. Add melted white chocolate mixture, flour, salt, and vanilla. Beat just until combined. Stir in the remaining chopped white chocolate and the chocolate pieces. Spoon mixture into the prepared pan.

3 Bake for 30 to 40 minutes or until evenly browned on top. Cool in pan on a wire rack for 20 minutes. Cut into bars.

For 20 brownies: Prepare using method above, except use an 8×8×2-inch baking pan.

PER BROWNIE: 160 cal., 8 g total fat (5 g sat. fat), 29 mg chol., 6 mg sodium, 20 g carbo., 1 g fiber, 2 g pro.

P.B. and Chocolate Fudge

Show gratitude to friends on your gift list by giving this incredibly divine yet easy to make chocolate confection.

1 For 128 servings, line a 13×9×2-inch baking pan with foil, extending the foil about 1 inch over the sides of pan. Butter the foil; set pan aside.

2 In a saucepan combine sugar and evaporated milk. Cook and stir over medium-high heat until mixture boils. Reduce heat to medium; cook and stir for 3 minutes more. Remove from heat.

3 Immediately stir peanut butter, marshmallow crème, and chocolate pieces into sugar mixture until chocolate pieces are melted and mixture is well combined. Quickly spread fudge evenly into the prepared pan. If desired, sprinkle with peanuts; lightly press peanuts into the fudge.

4 Cover and refrigerate for 2 to 3 hours or until firm. Remove fudge from pan, using the foil to lift. Place on cutting board; cut into bars. Store, covered, in the refrigerator up to 1 week.

For 64 servings: Prepare using method above, except use an 8×8×2-inch baking pan.

PER SERVING: 91 cal., 5 g total fat (1 g sat. fat), 1 mg chol., 35 mg sodium, 12 g carbo., 1 g fiber, 2 g pro.

PREP: 20 minutes
CHILL: 2 hours

128 servings	ingredients	64 servings
4 cups	sugar	2 cups
1 cup	evaporated milk	½ cup
1 28-oz. jar	creamy or chunky peanut butter	1 12-oz. jar
1 13-oz. jar	marshmallow crème	1 7-oz. jar
3 cups	semisweet chocolate pieces	1½ cups
1 cup	chopped peanuts (optional)	½ cup

Triple-Nut Zucchini Cake

Make this ooey-gooey treat in midsummer, when zucchini plants are producing generously.

1 Preheat oven to 350°F. For 20 servings, grease a 13×9×2-inch baking pan; set aside. In a 15×10×1-inch baking pan combine 1/2 cup of the walnuts, 1/2 cup of the pecans, 1/2 cup of the almonds, and the oats. Bake about 12 minutes or until toasted, stirring three times. Set aside on a wire rack.

2 Meanwhile, in a bowl combine flour, granulated sugar, baking powder, salt, and baking soda. Stir in zucchini, oil, egg(s), and vanilla until combined. Stir in toasted nut mixture. Spread batter evenly in prepared pan.

3 Bake for 30 to 40 minutes or until a wooden toothpick inserted near the center comes out clean. Cool in pan on a wire rack for 1 hour.

4 In a saucepan heat and stir butter and half-and-half over low heat until butter is melted. Add brown sugar; stir until sugar is dissolved. Remove from heat. Stir in the remaining nuts.

5 Preheat broiler and carefully adjust oven rack so cake will be 4 to 5 inches from heat. Spread butter and nut mixture over cake in pan. Broil for 1 1/2 to 2 minutes or until topping is bubbly and golden. Cool in pan on a wire rack for 1 hour before serving.

For 6 servings: Prepare using method above, except grease an 8×8×2-inch baking pan; set aside. In a 9×9×2-inch baking pan combine half the walnuts, half the pecans, half the almonds, and the oats.

PER SERVING: 386 cal., 24 g total fat (5 g sat. fat), 41 mg chol., 182 mg sodium, 42 g carbo., 2 g fiber, 4 g pro.

PREP: 25 minutes BAKE: 30 minutes
BROIL: 1 1/2 minutes COOL: 2 hours
OVEN: 350°F

20 servings	ingredients	9 servings
3/4 cup	chopped walnuts	1/4 cup
3/4 cup	chopped pecans	1/4 cup
3/4 cup	slivered almonds, chopped	1/4 cup
3/4 cup	rolled oats	1/4 cup
2 cups	all-purpose flour	2/3 cup
2 cups	granulated sugar	2/3 cup
1 tsp.	baking powder	1/4 tsp.
1 tsp.	salt	1/4 tsp.
1/4 tsp.	baking soda	1/8 tsp.
3 cups	shredded zucchini	1 cup
1 cup	vegetable oil	1/3 cup
3	egg(s), lightly beaten	1
1 tsp.	vanilla	1/4 tsp.
1/3 cup	butter	2 Tbsp.
3 Tbsp.	half-and-half, light cream, or milk	1 Tbsp.
2/3 cup	packed brown sugar	3 Tbsp.

Triple-Berry Pudding Cake

Having trouble deciding whether to bake berry shortcake, crisp, cobbler, or cake? Make this delectable dessert—it covers all the berry bases.

PREP: 25 minutes   BAKE: 40 minutes   BROIL: 1 minute
COOL: 30 minutes   OVEN: 350°F

16 servings	ingredients	8 servings
2 cups	fresh or frozen blueberries, thawed	1 cup
2 cups	fresh or frozen raspberries, thawed	1 cup
1 cup	cranberries	1/2 cup
2 cups	all-purpose flour	1 cup
1 1/3 cups	granulated sugar	2/3 cup
3 tsp.	baking powder	1 1/2 tsp.
1/2 tsp.	salt	1/4 tsp.
1 cup	milk	1/2 cup
1/4 cup	butter, melted	2 Tbsp.
2 tsp.	vanilla	1 tsp.
1 1/2 cups	boiling water	3/4 cup
2/3 cup	granulated sugar	1/3 cup
1 cup	sliced almonds	1/2 cup
2/3 cup	packed brown sugar	1/3 cup
1/2 cup	butter, melted	1/4 cup
	Ice cream (optional)	

1 Preheat oven to 350°F. For 16 servings, grease a 13×9×2-inch baking pan. Arrange blueberries, raspberries, and cranberries in prepared pan; set aside.

2 In a bowl combine flour, the 1 1/3 cups granulated sugar, baking powder, and salt. Add milk, the 1/4 cup melted butter, and vanilla; stir well. Spoon batter over berries in pan; carefully spread batter over berries.

3 In a bowl combine the boiling water and the 2/3 cup granulated sugar; pour evenly over batter. Bake for 40 to 50 minutes or until top is browned and edges are bubbly.

4 Meanwhile, in a bowl combine almonds, brown sugar, and the 1/2 cup melted butter.

5 Remove cake from oven. Preheat broiler and carefully adjust oven rack so cake will be 4 to 5 inches from heat. Spoon almond mixture evenly over cake. Broil for 1 to 2 minutes or just until top is golden. Cool on a wire rack for 30 minutes before serving. Spoon warm pudding cake into dessert dishes. If desired, serve with ice cream.

For 8 servings: Prepare using method above, except use a 9×9×2-inch baking pan.
   In Step 2 use 2/3 cup granulated sugar and 2 tablespoons melted butter.
   In Step 3 combine the boiling water and 1/3 cup granulated sugar.
   In Step 4 combine almonds, brown sugar, and the 1/4 cup melted butter.

PER SERVING: 335 cal., 14 g total fat (5 g sat. fat), 25 mg chol., 194 mg sodium, 50 g carbo., 4 g fiber, 4 g pro.

Gooey Butter Cake

Sometimes simplicity is utterly delicious. This richer-than-rich dessert is the perfect example.

1 Preheat oven to 350°F. For 24 servings, in a bowl combine the 2 cups flour and the ⅓ cup granulated sugar. Use a pastry blender to cut in ⅔ cup butter until mixture resembles fine crumbs and starts to cling. Pat butter mixture into the bottom of two 9×9×2-inch baking pans; set pans aside.

2 For filling, in a mixing bowl beat the 2½ cups granulated sugar and the 1½ cups softened butter with an electric mixer on medium speed until combined. Beat in corn syrup and egg(s) just until combined. Alternately add the 2 cups flour and evaporated milk to beaten sugar-butter mixture, beating just until combined after each addition. (Batter will appear slightly curdled.) Pour half the filling into each crust-lined baking pan.

3 Bake about 35 minutes or until each cake is nearly firm when you gently shake it. Cool in pans on wire racks. If you like, sift powdered sugar on each cake before serving.

For 12 servings: Prepare using method above, except in Step 1 combine 1 cup flour and the 3 tablespoons granulated sugar; cut in ⅓ cup butter. Use a 9×9×2-inch baking pan.

For filling, in Step 2 beat 1¼ cups granulated sugar and ¾ cup butter until combined. Add the 1 cup flour and evaporated milk alternately to beaten sugar-butter mixture, beating until just combined after each addition.

PER SERVING: 347 cal., 18 g total fat (11 g sat. fat), 5 mg chol., 142 mg sodium, 44 g carbo., 1 g fiber, 3 g pro.

PREP: 20 minutes   BAKE: 35 minutes
OVEN: 350°F

24 servings	ingredients	12 servings
2 cups	all-purpose flour	1 cup
⅓ cup	granulated sugar	3 Tbsp.
⅔ cup	butter	⅓ cup
2½ cups	granulated sugar	1¼ cups
1½ cups	butter, softened	¾ cup
½ cup	light-color corn syrup	¼ cup
2	egg(s)	1
2 cups	all-purpose flour	1 cup
2 5-oz. cans (1⅓ cups total)	evaporated milk	1 5-oz. can (⅔ cup)
Powdered sugar (optional)		

Banana Split Cake

Imagine all your favorite sundae's flavors in a cake! Serve this cozy indulgence slightly warm to garner the most oohs and ahhs.

**PREP: 20 minutes   BAKE: 35 minutes
COOL: 30 minutes   OVEN: 350°F**

16 servings	ingredients	9 servings
1 cup	butter	½ cup
4	eggs	2
3 cups	all-purpose flour	1½ cups
2 tsp.	baking powder	1 tsp.
1 tsp.	salt	½ tsp.
¼ tsp.	baking soda	⅛ tsp.
1½ cups	sugar	¾ cup
½ cup	mashed ripe banana	¼ cup
½ cup	sour cream	¼ cup
½ cup	milk	¼ cup
1 tsp.	vanilla	½ tsp.
½ cup	strawberry preserves	¼ cup
Few drops	red food coloring	Few drops
½ cup	presweetened cocoa powder (not low-calorie)	¼ cup
1 cup	chocolate fudge ice cream topping	½ cup
	Sliced bananas (optional)	
	Fresh strawberries (optional)	
	Maraschino cherries (optional)	
	Whipped cream (optional)	

1 Allow butter and eggs to stand at room temperature for 30 minutes. Preheat oven to 350°F. Grease and flour a 13×9×2-inch baking pan; set aside. In a bowl stir together flour, baking powder, salt, and baking soda; set aside.

2 In a bowl beat butter with an electric mixer on medium speed for 30 seconds. Gradually add sugar, beating well. Add eggs, one at a time, beating well after each addition. In a bowl combine banana, sour cream, milk, and vanilla. Alternately add flour mixture and banana mixture to butter mixture, beating on low speed after each addition.

3 In a small bowl stir together 1 cup of the batter, the strawberry preserves, and red food coloring. In another bowl stir together another 1 cup of the batter and the cocoa powder. Evenly spread all of the plain batter into the prepared pan. Spoon chocolate and strawberry batters in small mounds on the plain batter. Use a narrow metal spatula to swirl the batters.

4 Bake for 35 to 45 minutes or until a wooden toothpick inserted near the center comes out clean. Cool in pan on wire rack for 30 minutes.

5 In a saucepan heat ice cream topping until drizzling consistency. Serve cake with ice cream topping, bananas, strawberries, cherries, and whipped cream.

For 9 servings: Prepare using method above, except use a 9×9×2-inch baking pan. In Step 3 stir together ½ cup batter, strawberry preserves, and red food coloring. In another bowl stir together ½ cup batter and the cocoa powder.

PER SERVING: 410 cal., 17 g total fat (11 g sat. fat), 87 mg chol., 359 mg sodium, 60 g carbo., 1 g fiber, 4 g pro.

Best-Ever Chocolate Cake

Look no further. This absolutely perfect, decadent delight earns its name.

1 Allow the ¾ cup butter and eggs to stand at room temperature for 30 minutes. Preheat oven to 350°F. For 12 servings, lightly grease a 13×9×2-inch baking pan; set aside. In a bowl combine flour, cocoa powder, baking soda, baking powder, and salt.

2 In a mixing bowl beat softened butter with an electric mixer on medium speed for 30 seconds. Gradually add sugar, beating until combined. Continue beating on medium speed for 2 minutes more. Add eggs, one at a time, beating well after each addition. Beat in vanilla.

3 Alternately add flour mixture and milk to butter mixture, beating on low speed after each addition. Beat on medium speed for 20 seconds more. Spread batter into the prepared pan.

4 Bake for 35 to 40 minutes or until a wooden toothpick inserted near center comes out clean. Cool in pan on a wire rack for 1 hour.

5 For frosting, in a saucepan heat and stir chocolate pieces and the ¼ cup butter over low heat until combined. Remove from heat; cool 5 minutes. Stir in sour cream. Gradually add powdered sugar, beating with an electric mixer on low speed until smooth. Frost the top of the cake. If desired, serve with ice cream and raspberries.

For 9 servings: Prepare using method above, except allow ⅓ cup butter and eggs to stand at room temperature. Lightly grease a 9×9×2-inch baking pan. For frosting, in a saucepan heat and stir chocolate pieces and 2 tablespoons butter over low heat until combined.

PER SERVING: 360 cal., 15 g total fat (7 g sat. fat), 88 mg chol., 335 mg sodium, 51 g carbo., 1 g fiber, 6 g pro.

PREP: 20 minutes   BAKE: 35 minutes
COOL: 1 hour   OVEN: 350°F

12 servings	ingredients	9 servings
¾ cup	butter	⅓ cup
3	eggs	2
2 cups	all-purpose flour	1 cup
¾ cup	unsweetened cocoa powder	⅓ cup
1 tsp.	baking soda	½ tsp.
¾ tsp.	baking powder	¼ tsp.
½ tsp.	salt	¼ tsp.
2 cups	sugar	1 cup
2 tsp.	vanilla	1 tsp.
1½ cups	milk	¾ cup
1 cup	semisweet chocolate pieces	½ cup
¼ cup	butter	2 Tbsp.
½ cup	sour cream	¼ cup
2½ cups	powdered sugar	1¼ cups
	Ice cream (optional)	
	Fresh raspberries (optional)	

Crunchy Caramel Apple Cake

Make this chunky cake with any apple you enjoy eating out of hand. Granny Smith, Gala, Honey Crisp, and Sonja varieties all shine in this recipe.

PREP: 25 minutes
BAKE: 40 minutes
COOL: 1 hour
OVEN: 325°F

16 servings	ingredients	9 servings
1 cup	plain granola, crushed	1/2 cup
1 cup	chopped walnuts or pecans	1/2 cup
1/4 cup	butter, softened	2 Tbsp.
3 cups	all-purpose flour	1 1/2 cups
1 tsp.	baking soda	1/2 tsp.
1 tsp.	ground cinnamon	1/2 tsp.
1/2 tsp.	salt	1/4 tsp.
2	egg(s), lightly beaten	1
1 1/2 cups	vegetable oil	3/4 cup
1 cup	granulated sugar	1/2 cup
1 cup	packed brown sugar	1/2 cup
3 cups	finely chopped, peeled apples	1 1/2 cups
1/2 cup	butter	1/4 cup
1 cup	packed brown sugar	1/2 cup
1/2 cup	whipping cream	1/4 cup
1 tsp.	vanilla	1/2 tsp.
	Whipped cream (optional)	
	Chopped walnuts (optional)	

1 Preheat oven to 325°F. For 16 servings, grease a 13×9×2-inch baking pan; set aside. In a bowl combine granola and 1/2 cup of the nuts. Use your fingers or a fork to combine the 1/4 cup softened butter with granola mixture until crumbly; set aside.

2 In a bowl combine flour, baking soda, cinnamon, and salt; set aside. In another bowl combine eggs, oil, granulated sugar, and the 1 cup brown sugar. Add flour mixture; stir just until combined. Fold in apples and remaining nuts. Spoon batter into prepared pan, spreading evenly. Sprinkle with granola mixture.

3 Bake for 40 to 55 minutes or until a wooden toothpick inserted near the center comes out clean. Cool cake in pan on a wire rack 1 hour.

4 For sauce, in a saucepan melt the 1/2 cup butter over medium heat. Stir in the 1 cup packed brown sugar and whipping cream. Bring to boiling, stirring constantly; reduce heat. Simmer, uncovered, for 5 minutes or until mixture is slightly thickened. Remove from heat; stir in vanilla. Cool sauce 10 minutes. Serve warm over cake. If desired, serve with whipped cream and walnuts.

For 9 servings: Prepare using method above, except grease a 9×9×2-inch baking pan. In Step 1 use 1/4 cup of the nuts and 2 tablespoons softened butter. In Step 2 combine eggs, oil, granulated sugar, and the 1/2 cup brown sugar. In Step 4 melt the 1/4 cup butter. Stir in 1/2 cup packed brown sugar and whipping cream.

PER SERVING: 630 cal., 39 g total fat (10 g sat. fat), 61 mg chol., 240 mg sodium, 68 g carbo., 3 g fiber, 6 g pro.

Cherry Cobbler

Whip up this sweet classic when you crave a bowl of pure comfort. Fresh or frozen fruit makes the dessert easy to serve year-round.

PREP: 25 minutes
BAKE: 20 minutes
OVEN: 400°F

12 servings	ingredients	6 servings
2 cups	all-purpose flour	1 cup
1/4 cup	sugar	2 Tbsp.
3 tsp.	baking powder	1 1/2 tsp.
1/2 tsp.	salt	1/4 tsp.
1/4 cup	butter or margarine	2 Tbsp.
12 cups	fresh or frozen unsweetened pitted tart red cherries	6 cups
2 cups	sugar	1 cup
1/4 cup	cornstarch	2 Tbsp.
2	egg(s), lightly beaten	1
1/2 cup	milk	1/4
	Vanilla ice cream (optional)	

1 Preheat oven to 400°F. For 12 servings, for topping, in a bowl combine flour, the 1/4 cup sugar, the baking powder, and salt. Using a pastry blender, cut in butter until mixture resembles coarse crumbs; set aside.

2 For filling, in a saucepan combine the cherries, the 2 cups sugar, and the cornstarch. Cook over medium heat until cherries juice out, stirring occasionally. Cook and stir over medium heat until thickened and bubbly. Keep filling hot.

3 In a bowl stir together eggs and milk. Add egg mixture to flour mixture, stirring just to moisten. Transfer hot filling to a 3-quart rectangular baking dish. Using a spoon, immediately drop topping in 12 mounds on filling.

4 Bake, uncovered, for 20 to 30 minutes or until topping is golden brown. Serve warm. If desired, serve with ice cream.

For 6 servings: Prepare using method above, except in Step 1 combine flour with 2 tablespoons sugar.

In Step 2 combine the cherries, the 1 cup sugar, and the cornstarch.

In Step 3 transfer hot filling to a 2-quart square baking dish and drop topping in six mounds on filling.

PER SERVING: 386 cal., 10 g total fat (5 g sat. fat), 58 mg chol., 236 mg sodium, 73 g carbo., 3 g fiber, 5 g pro.

Orange-Chocolate Bread Pudding

Complex flavors in bittersweet chocolate deliver pure chocolate pleasure in every bite of this warm dessert.

PREP: 25 minutes   BAKE: 45 minutes
COOL: 30 minutes   OVEN: 325F°

8 servings	ingredients	4 servings
	Butter	
8 cups	1-inch French or Italian bread cubes	4 cups
4 cups	milk	2 cups
1 cup	sugar	½ cup
6 oz.	bittersweet chocolate, coarsely chopped	3 oz.
8	eggs, lightly beaten	4
1 Tbsp.	finely shredded orange peel	1½ tsp.
1 tsp.	vanilla	½ tsp.
⅛ tsp.	salt	Dash
	Whipped cream (optional)	

1 Preheat oven to 325°F. For 8 servings, butter a 3-quart rectangular baking dish. Place bread cubes in the dish, spreading evenly. Set aside.

2 In a saucepan combine milk, sugar, and chocolate. Cook and stir over medium heat until the chocolate is melted. Remove from heat; cool slightly.

3 In a bowl combine eggs, orange peel, vanilla, and salt. Gradually whisk in the chocolate mixture. Carefully pour mixture over bread in prepared dish. Press lightly with back of spoon to moisten all bread cubes.

4 Bake, uncovered, for 45 to 50 minutes or until evenly puffed and set. Cool on a wire rack for 30 minutes before serving. Serve warm. If desired, serve with whipped cream.

For 4 servings: Prepare using method above, except butter a 2-quart square baking dish.

PER SERVING: 434 cal., 18 g total fat (9 g sat. fat), 226 mg chol., 351 mg sodium, 59 g carbo., 2 g fiber, 16 g pro.

Rhubarb Surprise Crisp

Spring's first treats—sweet strawberries and tart rhubarb—marry in a simple, old-fashioned dessert. Serve it slightly warm for the best effect.

1 Preheat oven to 375°F. For 12 servings, in a bowl combine the granulated sugar, cornstarch, and cinnamon. (For fresh rhubarb, use 4 teaspoons cornstarch. For frozen, use 6 teaspoons cornstarch.) Stir in rhubarb, strawberries, and basil. Spoon fruit mixture into a 3-quart rectangular baking dish, spreading evenly; set aside.

2 For topping, in another bowl combine flour, oats, brown sugar, and salt. Stir in melted butter. Evenly sprinkle topping on fruit mixture.

3 Bake, uncovered, for 30 to 40 minutes or until fruit is tender and topping is golden brown. Serve warm. If desired, serve with sweetened whipped cream.

For 6 servings: Prepare using method above, except for fresh rhubarb, use 2 teaspoons cornstarch; for frozen, use 3 teaspoons cornstarch. Spoon into a 2-quart square baking dish, spreading evenly; set aside.

PER SERVING: 281 cal., 7 g total fat (4 g sat. fat), 15 mg chol., 144 mg sodium, 54 g carbo., 3 g fiber, 3 g pro.

**PREP: 20 minutes   BAKE: 30 minutes
OVEN: 375°F**

12 servings	ingredients	6 servings
1⅓ cups	granulated sugar	⅔ cup
4 or 6 tsp.	cornstarch	2 or 3 tsp.
½ tsp.	ground cinnamon	¼ tsp.
4 cups	sliced fresh rhubarb or frozen unsweetened sliced rhubarb, thawed	2 cups
4 cups	coarsely chopped fresh strawberries	2 cups
¼ cup	snipped fresh basil	2 Tbsp.
1 cup	all-purpose flour	½ cup
1 cup	quick-cooking rolled oats	½ cup
⅔ cup	packed brown sugar	⅓ cup
½ tsp.	salt	¼ tsp.
⅓ cup	butter, melted	3 Tbsp.
	Sweetened whipped cream (optional)	

Apple-Cranberry Dessert

Fresh cranberries are available only a short time, but they freeze beautifully. Buy a few extra bags and freeze them to use year-round.

PREP: 10 minutes
BAKE: 1 hour
COOL: 30 minutes
OVEN: 325°F

12 servings	ingredients	6 servings
2 12-oz. pkg.	fresh cranberries	1 12-oz. pkg.
2 cups	chopped, peeled, cored cooking apple	1 cup
2 Tbsp.	butter, cut up	1 Tbsp.
1¹/₃ cups	sugar	²/₃ cup
1 cup	chopped walnuts or pecans	¹/₂ cup
2	egg(s), lightly beaten	1
²/₃ cup	butter, melted	¹/₃ cup
1 cup	sugar	¹/₂ cup
²/₃ cup	all-purpose flour	¹/₃ cup
	Vanilla ice cream	

1 Preheat oven to 325°F. For 12 servings, grease the bottom of a 13×9×2-inch baking pan. Toss the cranberries and apple together in the prepared pan. Dot cranberry mixture with the 2 tablespoons butter. Evenly sprinkle with the 1¹/₃ cups sugar and the walnuts. Set aside.

2 In a bowl whisk together the eggs and the ²/₃ cup melted butter. Stir in the 1 cup sugar and flour, whisking until well combined. Evenly pour egg mixture over cranberry mixture.

3 Bake, uncovered, about 1 hour or until top is golden brown and filling is bubbly. Cool on a wire rack for 30 minutes before serving. Serve warm or at room temperature with vanilla ice cream.

For 6 servings: Prepare using method above, except grease the bottom of an 8×8×2-inch baking pan. Dot cranberry mixture with the 1 tablespoon butter. Sprinkle evenly with the ²/₃ cup sugar and the walnuts. In Step 2 whisk together the egg and the ¹/₃ cup melted butter. Stir in the ¹/₂ cup sugar and the flour, whisking until well combined.

PER SERVING: 540 cal., 27 g total fat (13 g sat. fat), 99 mg chol., 157 mg sodium, 72 g carbo., 4 g fiber, 6 g pro.

INDEX

Metric Information

The charts on this page provide a guide for converting measurements from the U.S. customary system, which is used throughout this book, to the metric system.

Product Differences

Most of the ingredients called for in the recipes in this book are available in most countries. However, some are known by different names. Here are some common American ingredients and their possible counterparts:

- Sugar (white) is granulated, fine granulated, or castor sugar.
- Powdered sugar is icing sugar.
- All-purpose flour is enriched, bleached or unbleached white household flour. When self-rising flour is used in place of all-purpose flour in a recipe that calls for leavening, omit the leavening agent (baking soda or baking powder) and salt.
- Light-color corn syrup is golden syrup.
- Cornstarch is cornflour.
- Baking soda is bicarbonate of soda.
- Vanilla or vanilla extract is vanilla essence.
- Green, red, or yellow sweet peppers are capsicums or bell peppers.
- Golden raisins are sultanas.

Volume and Weight

The United States traditionally uses cup measures for liquid and solid ingredients. The chart below shows the approximate imperial and metric equivalents. If you are accustomed to weighing solid ingredients, the following approximate equivalents will be helpful.

- 1 cup butter, castor sugar, or rice = 8 ounces = $1/2$ pound = 250 grams
- 1 cup flour = 4 ounces = $1/4$ pound = 125 grams
- 1 cup icing sugar = 5 ounces = 150 grams

Canadian and U.S. volume for a cup measure is 8 fluid ounces (237 ml), but the standard metric equivalent is 250 ml.

1 British imperial cup is 10 fluid ounces.

In Australia, 1 tablespoon equals 20 ml, and there are 4 teaspoons in the Australian tablespoon.

Spoon measures are used for smaller amounts of ingredients. Although the size of the tablespoon varies slightly in different countries, for practical purposes and for recipes in this book, a straight substitution is all that's necessary. Measurements made using cups or spoons always should be level unless stated otherwise.

Common Weight Range Replacements

Imperial / U.S.	Metric
$1/2$ ounce	15 g
1 ounce	25 g or 30 g
4 ounces ($1/4$ pound)	115 g or 125 g
8 ounces ($1/2$ pound)	225 g or 250 g
16 ounces (1 pound)	450 g or 500 g
$1 1/4$ pounds	625 g
$1 1/2$ pounds	750 g
2 pounds or $2 1/4$ pounds	1,000 g or 1 Kg

Oven Temperature Equivalents

Fahrenheit Setting	Celsius Setting*	Gas Setting
300°F	150°C	Gas Mark 2 (very low)
325°F	160°C	Gas Mark 3 (low)
350°F	180°C	Gas Mark 4 (moderate)
375°F	190°C	Gas Mark 5 (moderate)
400°F	200°C	Gas Mark 6 (hot)
425°F	220°C	Gas Mark 7 (hot)
450°F	230°C	Gas Mark 8 (very hot)
475°F	240°C	Gas Mark 9 (very hot)
500°F	260°C	Gas Mark 10 (extremely hot)
Broil	Broil	Grill

*Electric and gas ovens may be calibrated using celsius. However, for an electric oven, increase celsius setting 10 to 20 degrees when cooking above 160°C. For convection or forced air ovens (gas or electric), lower the temperature setting 25°F/10°C when cooking at all heat levels.

Baking Pan Sizes

Imperial / U.S.	Metric
9×$1^1/2$-inch round cake pan	22- or 23×4-cm (1.5 L)
9×$1^1/2$-inch pie plate	22- or 23×4-cm (1 L)
8×8×2-inch square cake pan	20×5-cm (2 L)
9×9×2-inch square cake pan	22- or 23×4.5-cm (2.5 L)
11×7×$1^1/2$-inch baking pan	28×17×4-cm (2 L)
2-quart rectangular baking pan	30×19×4.5-cm (3 L)
13×9×2-inch baking pan	34×22×4.5-cm (3.5 L)
15×10×1-inch jelly roll pan	40×25×2-cm
9×5×3-inch loaf pan	23×13×8-cm (2 L)
2-quart casserole	2 L

U.S. / Standard Metric Equivalents

$1/8$ teaspoon = 0.5 ml	
$1/4$ teaspoon = 1 ml	
$1/2$ teaspoon = 2 ml	
1 teaspoon = 5 ml	
1 tablespoon = 15 ml	
2 tablespoons = 25 ml	
$1/4$ cup = 2 fluid ounces = 50 ml	
$1/3$ cup = 3 fluid ounces = 75 ml	
$1/2$ cup = 4 fluid ounces = 125 ml	
$2/3$ cup = 5 fluid ounces = 150 ml	
$3/4$ cup = 6 fluid ounces = 175 ml	
1 cup = 8 fluid ounces = 250 ml	
2 cups = 1 pint = 500 ml	
1 quart = 1 litre	